JN023553

外国人とわかりあうために

英語で伝える日本のマナー

Manners and conventions of daily life in Japan

小笠原敬承斎

Keishosai Ogasawara

淡交社

はじめに

　日本はどのようなところなのだろう。

　日本人はどのようなことを重んじるのだろう。

　日本に住んでいても、日本人同士、互いに相手のこころを理解することは難しいときがあります。とはいうものの世界中、どの国の人であっても相手のこころを全て読むことは難しいのではないでしょうか。

　しかし、せっかく日本を訪れるのであれば、あるいは日本に住むのであれば、できるだけ相手とのこころの温度差をなくして、互いに快適な空間のなかで幸せに過ごしたいと思いませんか。そこで、日本の作法の根底にある理由を知ることによって、古来受け継がれてきた日本人のこころを理解いただきたいのです。この願いは、外国人だけでなく、現代社会に生きる日本人に対しても同様に感じています。

　さて、外国映画に日本人が登場するたび、なぜ日本人は相手と挨拶をするときに何度もお辞儀をするのだろうかということを残念に思います。その姿を情けなく感じることさえあります。海外の方から、この姿が日本の正しい挨拶の仕方とは思っていただきたくはありません。

　何度もお辞儀をするのではなく、挨拶時には一回のお辞儀にこころを込めて行うことが重要です。何度もお辞儀をする姿は、相手の目に卑屈に映ることがあります。お辞儀の数が多くなればなるほど、それぞれのお辞儀は軽くなり、ゆえに相手を軽んじていることにも繋がりかねないので、できるかぎり避けるべきです。

Preface

What is Japan like?
What is it that Japanese people value?

Even among Japanese people, sometimes it is difficult to fully understand what another person is feeling. This may not only be the case for Japan. Construing others minds is difficult anywhere around the globe.

That said, if you would have an opportunity to visit or live in Japan, wouldn't it be wonderful to have a harmonious time and space for you and others by trying to understand where the other person is coming from? I hope this book will help you to learn the underlying reasons for Japanese manners that leads to an understanding of the hearts and minds of Japanese people based on cultural attitudes that have been handed down from ancient times. My hope goes out not only for people from overseas, but also Japanese people living in modern times.

We often see scenes in foreign films in which a Japanese person bows repeatedly to greet others, it can even feel pathetic at times. It is my strong hope to correct the stereotypes among non-Japanese viewers.

When greeting, instead of bowing many times, it is important to bow once with warm intensions. Bowing more than once may appear obsequious to the receiver's eyes. When bowing more than once, each bow loses its meaning and it gives the impression that you are taking someone lightly. So we should avoid it as much as possible.

Moreover, it is not ideal that you speak the words of greeting while

また、挨拶に用いることばをお辞儀と同時に口にすることは望ましくありません。「おはようございます」と明るく挨拶をしているつもりが、ことばを述べながらお辞儀をすると顔を下に向けてしまうために、どことなく暗い印象を与えてしまうことも考えられます。したがって、相手に視線を合わせてことばを述べてからお辞儀をする。またはお辞儀をしてから相手に視線を合わせてことばを述べる。いずれかの方法をとることで、お辞儀とことばの両方にしっかりとこころを込めることができます。

　改まった場において丁寧に挨拶をするときは、お辞儀をしてからもとの姿勢にもどり、「○○と申します。本日は○○様とお目にかかることができ、誠に光栄に存じます」などと口上を述べ、再度お辞儀をいたします。

　このように、挨拶ひとつとっても、状況に応じて臨機応変に行動することが大切です。それには、「なぜ」（に対する理由）が必要不可欠です。「なぜ」を学ぶことで、基本を身につけることができるからです。

　日常の「なぜ」を通じてこころの扉を開き、豊かな日々をお過ごしになってみてはいかがですか。

bowing. You may mean well and think you are greeting in a light-hearted manner, but you are actually facing downward when speaking and it might give a gloomy impression. It is best to speak your greeting with eye contact, followed by a bow, or the other way around. This way, you are able to be mindful in both actions, bowing and greeting.

For a formal greeting, you are expected to bow first and share your greeting, such as "it's such an honor to meet you, Mr./ Ms. xx", after returning to the original position, then bow again.

The point is that it is especially important when it comes to Japanese greetings to act upon the time and circumstances. In order to be able to do so, we need to understand the motives. Learning why we do things certain ways will help us to get grounded in basics.

I hope these explorations open the door to your mind and help you to have a meaningful experience in Japan.

もくじ

はじめに   2

i   ビジネスシーンの「なぜ」—— 13

1 なぜ「おつかれさまです」「お世話になっております」「よろしくお願いいたします」などの挨拶のことばをあらゆる場面で用いるのですか？ —— 14

2 なぜ天気の話題から会話が始まることが多いのですか？ —— 18

3 上司の名前を呼ばずに「部長」などと役職で呼ぶのはなぜですか？ —— 20

4 なぜ「貴社」「弊社」というのですか？ 自分のことは何といえばよいのでしょうか？ —— 22

5 約束の時間の前に到着するほうがよいのでしょうか？ —— 24

6 応接室、車内、電車内などでどのあたりに座るのがよいのでしょうか？ —— 26

7 名刺の交換の仕方に決まりがあるのですか？ —— 30

8 仕事の関係者になぜおみやげを持参するのですか？ —— 34

9 本音と建て前、どのように理解したらよいのでしょうか？ —— 36

10 訪問のアポイントメントを取る際に心得ておくべきことはありますか？ その理由は？ また、おいとまに関する心得は？ —— 40

ii   お宅訪問したときの「なぜ」—— 45

11 相手の家には、早めに到着してもよいのでしょうか？ —— 46

Contents

Preface   *3*

I   Business Occasions — 13

1.   Why do Japanese people usually greet others with *Otsukare-sama* "Good job", *Osewani natte-orimasu* "Thank you for your acquaintance", or *Yoroshiku onegai shimasu* "Please do me the favor"? — *15*

2.   Why do Japanese people start conversations with the topic of the weather? — *19*

3.   Why do Japanese people call their supervisor by the job title and not their name? — *21*

4.   Why do Japanese people use *kisha* for a company with which they do business and *heisha* for their own company? How should I refer to myself? — *23*

5.   Is it better to arrive early for an appointment? — *25*

6.   Where should I be seated in a meeting room, a car, or on the train? — *27*

7.   What do I need to know about exchanging name cards? — *31*

8.   Why do Japanese people bring souvenirs to business partners? — *35*

9.   How can I know one's *honne* "real intention" and *tatemae* "what one says on the surface"? — *37*

10.   What should I know about making an appointment for a visit? How about when I leave? — *41*

II   Visiting Private Homes — 45

11.   Is it OK to arrive at someone's house before the expected time? — *47*

12 家に入る前にコートや帽子は取りますか？ —————— 48

13 玄関で靴を脱ぐときは、どうしたらよいのでしょうか？ —— 50

14 おみやげには、どのようなものを準備したらよいです
か？ おみやげを渡すとき、なぜ「つまらないものですが」—— 54
というのでしょう？ 紙袋のままで渡してよいですか？

15 座る場所に決まりがあるのですか？ ——————— 58

16 正座は足が痛くて無理。どうしても正座しなくてはだめ —— 62
ですか？ 楽に正座する方法はありますか？

iii 旅館や和食店での「なぜ」—— 67

17 床の間に関する決まりごとはありますか？ ————— 68

18 和室でしてはいけないことはありますか？ ————— 72

19 和食の席で心得ておくことはありますか？ ————— 78

20 箸の持ち方や箸の素材に決まりはありますか？ ——— 82

21 避けたほうがよい箸遣いについて、教えてください。—— 86

22 食事中、とくに注意すべきことは、ほかにありますか？—— 90

23 箸を休めるときはどうすればよいですか？ ————— 94

24 椀の蓋の扱い方を教えてください。 ——————— 98

25 お酒を酌み交わすときの決まりはありますか？ ——— 102

26 抹茶を飲むときに茶椀を回さないといけないのはなぜ —— 106
ですか？

27 大浴場での決まりを教えてください。——————— 108

28 日本ではチップは必要ないと聞いたけれど、「こころづ —— 112
け」とは何ですか？

12 | Should I take off my coat and hat before entering someone's home? —— 49

13 | What do I need to know about taking off my shoes? —— 51

14 | What should I bring as a souvenir? Why do Japanese people say *Tsumaranai mono desuga* "It's nothing special but I hope you like it" when handing over souvenirs? Should I give a souvenir with or without the paper bag? —— 55

15 | Where should I be seated? —— 59

16 | *Seiza* "sitting on one's knees" is painful. Is it unavoidable? Is there a trick to make it any easier? —— 63

Visiting *Ryokan* and Japanese Restaurants

—— 67

17 | What is the alcove and what do I need to know about it? —— 69

18 | What are some taboo behaviors in Japanese style rooms? —— 73

19 | What do I need to know about dining at Japanese restaurants? —— 79

20 | What do I need to know about chopsticks? —— 83

21 | Are there any taboos related to the use of chopsticks? —— 87

22 | What do I need to know while I am dining at a Japanese restaurant? —— 91

23 | What do I need to know when I want to put down my chopsticks? —— 95

24 | What do I need to know to handle a bowl lid? —— 99

25 | What do I need to know about drinking manners? —— 103

26 | Why do I need to turn the tea bowl when drinking *matcha*? —— 107

27 | What do I need to know about public baths? —— 109

28 | I hear people don't tip in Japan. What is *kokoro zuke*? —— 113

iv 冠婚葬祭の「なぜ」 ——— 117

29 「冠婚葬祭」って何ですか？ とくに「冠」がわかりにくいので教えてください。 ——— 118

30 日本の結婚式の決まりごとを教えてください。 ——— 122

31 結婚祝いに関する心得を教えてください。また、披露宴に伺う際、気をつけることはありますか？ ——— 128

32 日本の葬式について教えてください。通夜と告別式とは違うのですか。 ——— 132

33 葬式のときの服装について教えてください。 ——— 136

34 焼香、玉串、献花について教えてください。 ——— 138

35 通夜や告別式にはお金を持参するのですか？ ——— 142

36 「神仏習合」とは何ですか。神社と寺院を参拝する際に違いはありますか？ ——— 144

V 年中行事の「なぜ」 ——— 151

正月 ——— 152

五節供 ——— 156

節分 ——— 160

彼岸（春・秋） ——— 162

盆 ——— 162

中元 ——— 164

月見 ——— 164

七五三 ——— 166

歳暮 ——— 166

すす払い ——— 168

着物、浴衣について ——— 170

IV Ceremonial Occasions ——————— 117

29 | What does *kan-kon-so-sai* "ceremonial occasions" mean in Japan? — 119

30 | What do I need to know about Japanese weddings? ——————— 123

31 | What do I need to know about a wedding gift or when attending reception parties? ——— 129

32 | What do I need to know about Japanese funerals? What is the difference between a wake and funeral? ——— 133

33 | What should I wear to a funeral? ——————————— 137

34 | What do I need to know about manners at funerals? ————— 139

35 | Should we bring gift money to a wake or funeral? ————— 143

36 | What is syncretism? What do I need to know about visiting shrines and temples? ——— 145

V Annual Festivals ——————— 151

Shogatsu ————————————————————— 153

Go-sekku ————————————————————— 157

Setsubun ————————————————————— 161

Higan —————————————————————— 163

Bon ——————————————————————— 163

Chugen ————————————————————— 165

Tsuki-mi ————————————————————— 167

Shichi-go-san ———————————————————— 167

Seibo —————————————————————— 169

Susu harai ———————————————————— 169

Kimono & Yukata ——————————————————— 171

ビジネスシーンの
「なぜ」

なぜ「おつかれさまです」「お世話になって
おります」「よろしくお願いいたします」などの
挨拶のことばをあらゆる場面で用いるのですか?

日本では、同僚とすれ違うとき、相手が席に戻ったとき、電話で話すとき、あらゆる場面で「おつかれさま」といいます。「おつかれさま」は相手をねぎらうことばですが、このようにねぎらいの意味のほか、**挨拶の慣用句**のようにも用いられます。相手と行きあうときに何もいわないで通りすぎてもよいところを、あえて「おつかれさま」ということで相手への思いやりを表現しようとするわけです。電話でも会話の最初に「おつかれさまです」と返すことが一般的です。

「お世話になっております」も様々な場面で使われます。たとえば、メールの書き出しにも「お世話になっております」と記すことがありますが、この一文があることによって丁寧さが増し、いきなり本文に入るよりもやわらかい印象をつくります。昨今、こうした挨拶文は必要なく無意味であるとする意見がありますが、用件のみを記すのではなく、**相手への感謝や敬意を最初に伝える慣習は失くしたくないものです。**

「よろしくお願いいたします」は、目的や意図がなくても用いられる曖昧な表現です。「お取りはからいください」という意味も持ちます。またこちらが何か便宜を図ってほしい場合、具体的に全てをことばにしなくても、相手は「よろしくお願いいたします」からこころを読み取ります。互いに気持ちを察するわけです。その一方で「ご指導のほど、よろしくお願い申しあげます」などと、本来は具体的に何をお願いした

Why do Japanese people usually greet others with *Otsukare-sama* "Good job", *Osewani natte-orimasu* "Thank you for your acquaintance", or *Yoroshiku onegai shimasu* "Please do me the favor"?

In Japan, people use *Otsukare-sama* for all sorts of business occasions, such as passing your colleagues in the hallway, acknowledging they are back at their seats or starting a conversation on a phone call. It is literally translated as "good job" but it actually means "How are you?" or "How's it going?" Instead of passing somebody silently, saying *Otsukare-sama* is a way to show your care for that person. At some point, it became a norm to start a phone conversation with *Otsukare-sama desu*.

Osewani natte-orimasu is also used at various occasions. Often, people start emails with this phrase. It adds a sense of politeness to your email and gives a soft impression rather than starting bluntly with the subject. Lately, some people find these greetings to be unnecessary and pointless in business emails, but it would be a shame to see the custom to address our gratitude and respect to others disappear and our manners become too straightforward.

Yoroshiku onegai shimasu is an ambiguous expression you can use for many occasions and with differing intent. For instance, it could mean "Thank you for your arrangement." When you are asking someone a favor, instead of spelling out everything, if you say *Yoroshiku onegai shimasu*, the other person will understand what you are implying. Through a phrase like this, Japanese people consider the hearts of others. That said, in principle, it might be better to be more specific

いのかということを加えるほうが基本的には好ましいともいえましょう。「よろしくお願いいたします」というと、相手が「こちらこそよろしくお願いいたします」などと返すことも多くあります。

　このように、日本人は挨拶の際にいくつかの決まった表現をします。いずれにしても、農耕民族であったことから協調性を欠かすことができず、仲間や周囲との「和」を重んじる文化が根底にあり、たったひとことからでも人間関係を円滑にしたいと思う気持ちが働きます。そのことばは直接的でなく、曖昧ともとれる表現だからこそ、機微に聡くありたいとこころを積極的に働かせ、好ましい人間関係を育むのです。

about what you are asking when you can. e.g. *Goshido no hodo yoroshi-ku onegai moushiage-masu.* "Thank you for your supervision." When greeted with *Yoroshiku onegai shimasu*, it is common to greet back with *Kochira koso, yoroshiku onegai shimasu* "I thank you too."

As you can see, Japanese people use certain phrases for certain occasions. This comes from our historically agricultural background and how cooperation and working in harmony have been essential for survival. Having a group-oriented culture, Japanese people wish to facilitate relationships smoothly even in their words of greeting. Also, using ambiguous expressions, instead of being direct, contributes to the ability to surmise other's intent, which helps build successful relationships.

なぜ天気の話題から
会話が始まることが多いのですか？

出張先で駅からタクシーに乗ると、「どちらからいらしたのですか。こちらは寒いでしょう。今日は朝から雪が降っているのですよ」などと話しかけられます。

ホテルで案内係の人と客室に向かうまでの間、「今日は雨ですが、明日は晴れの予報です」と教えていただきます。マンションで今まで会ったことのない住人とエレベーターで一緒になったら、「久しぶりによい天気ですね」と声をかけます。

このように、特に初めて会った人との会話において、天気を話題にすることはめずらしくありません。

なぜ、天気の話題が多いかというと、誰でもがわかることだからです。携帯電話を持っていれば、天気はすぐに調べることができますし、新聞やテレビ番組でも天気予報は簡単に見ることができます。しかも同じ場所にいれば、一緒にそのときの気候を体験しているわけですから、それが相手と共通する話題になるのです。

相手とどの程度、こころの距離を保ったらよいのかがわからないうちは、相手に失礼がない話題で会話をすることで、その後の接し方を理解するきっかけにもなります。

四季のある日本において、**人々は天候の移り変わりから様々なことを学び**、農作業に活かしていました。その四季の移ろいこそが日本文化を支えてきたといっても過言ではないでしょう。

Why do Japanese people start conversations with the topic of the weather?

When you take a taxi on your business trip, the driver often starts the conversation with something like "Where are you from? It's cold here, isn't it? It's been snowing since this morning."

At a hotel, your porter may tell you "Today it's raining but the forecast says tomorrow will be fine." If you share an elevator in your apartment with another resident who you don't know, you might say something like "It's finally a nice day".

In Japan, it is quite common to start a conversation with someone you meet for the first time, taking about the weather.

This is because the weather is something everyone shares. You can easily look up weather forecasts with your mobile phone if you didn't read it in a newspaper or see it on TV. Or if you are in the same space, you obviously are experiencing the same weather so it can be a common subject.

Until you have a sense of another person's comfort zone, it is best to talk about general subjects to avoid coming across as rude. By talking about general topics, you can also assess how you might approach that person later.

Having four distinctive seasons in Japan, people have learnt a great deal from the weather and adapted that knowledge to their agricultural practices. It may not be an exaggeration to say it is the transitions of the four seasons that has shaped Japanese culture.

上司の名前を呼ばずに「部長」などと
役職で呼ぶのはなぜですか?

最近、上司に対してその役職ではなく「○○さん」とさんをつけて名前を呼ぶことを推奨している会社もありますが、日本には相手を名前ではなく、役職のみで呼ぶ慣習があります。

その慣習は今に始まったことではなく、古来より存在していました。たとえば、平安時代において、源氏物語の作者・紫式部は本名ではなく呼称です。本名は不明とされています。

鎌倉時代から江戸時代においても、相手の名前を気軽に呼ぶことは失礼であるとされていました。なぜなら、名前に限らず、ことばは声に発することにより霊力を持つとされていたからです。特に社会的地位の高い人の名を呼ぶことは畏れ多いとされ、武家社会においては、諱（いみな、生前の実名）と字（あざな、あだなのこと）があるなかで、相手を呼ぶときは本名を避けて、役職名や幼名、字で呼んでいました。つまり、**名前（本名）はその人の人格そのもの**と考えられていたわけです。

このような慣習が現代にまで伝えられ、役職のみで呼ぶことが相手に対する敬意の表現とされているのです。

また役職で呼ばれることは、その役職にある人自身の仕事に対する責任感を育てるともいわれています。公私を分けるためにも、「○○さん」ではなく役職を呼ぶことによって、自然とお互いの立場を重んじながら仕事ができるのではないかと思います。

Why do Japanese people call their supervisor by the job title and not their name?

Lately, some Japanese companies recommend calling your supervisors by their names instead of their job titles. But traditionally, it has been a custom to call them by their positions.

People have been doing so since ancient times. The well-known story *The Tale of Genji* from the Heian period (794 – 1185) was written by Murasaki Shikibu. Murasaki Shikibu means Lady Murasaki and it is her designation and not real name. Her real name is said to be unknown.

In the Kamakura (1185 – 1333) and Edo periods (1603 – 1868), it was believed to be too casual and even rude to call someone by their name, because people thought, not just names, but any word gains some psychic power when being pronounced. Calling someone with high social status by their names was considered especially disrespectful. Also, *samurai* often had their real names and courtesy names. People didn't go by their real names, but used their official positions, childhood names or courtesy names. Real names were thought to be very personal.

Such customs have been passed down to modern times and calling someone by their job titles is a way to show one's respect to their seniors at work.

In addition, people believe calling someone by their job title would foster the sense of responsibility that person carries with their position. Calling someone by their job title instead of their name helps to draw a line between public and private affairs and to commit to one's work while respecting each other's positions.

4

なぜ「貴社」「弊社」というのですか？
自分のことは何といえばよいのでしょうか？

相手の会社を貴社と呼ぶのは、**その会社を敬（うやま）っている表現**だからであり、失礼がないようにとのこころ遣いからです。「貴」は、とうとい、身分が高いなどの意味を示します。同じ意味で「御社」がありますが、一般的に、「貴社」は文書に、「御社」は口語で用います。

相手を敬うことから自分や自分の側をへりくだって表現することがあります。「弊社」はその代表的なものです。丁寧な表現ですが、社内の人同士で用いるのは不自然ですので、その場合は「当社」と表現するとよいでしょう。

また、「弊社」は文書、「当社」は口語に使うことが基本であるとの考え方もあるようですが、「当社」にはへりくだった意味が含まれていないので、口語でも弊社を用いるほうが好ましいと思います。

個人に関しては、自分のことを「小生（しょうせい）」「小職（しょうしょく）」などというへりくだった表現がありますが、若い世代の人が用いると背伸びをしている印象を与えることもあり、すべての職業や口語には適さない表現です。

また自分のことを苗字で呼ぶ人は自己顕示欲が強い、名前で呼ぶ人は幼いなどともいわれます。ビジネスシーンはもちろんのこと、日常において**自分のことを指すときは「私」を用いる**ことをおすすめいたします。

相手の名前をそのまま呼ぶことを「呼び捨て」といいますが、プライベートにおいても相手の名前には「さん」をつけることが基本です。

Why do Japanese people use *kisha* for a company with which they do business and *heisha* for their own company? How should I refer to myself?

The *kanji* character 貴 *(ki)* means noble and calling your business partner company *kisha*（貴社）is a way to show your respect to them. *Onsha*（御社）has the same meaning but generally, *kisha* is used in writing and *onsha* is for speaking.

In Japan, in order to show respect to others, people sometime humble themselves. *Heisha*（弊社）is a good example of that. It is a polite form of referring to your own company, but it would not be appropriate to use it among colleagues from the same company. You should use *tosha*（当社）in that case.

Some use *heisha* in writing and *tosha* for speaking but *tosha* doesn't have a sense of humility and it is ideal to use *heisha* in both writing and speaking when referring to your own company.

When it comes to referring to oneself, there are humbling expressions such as *shosei*（小生）or *shoushoku*（小職）but if used by younger people, it may give an impression of trying too hard. Also, they are not suitable for all kinds of occupations, or in speaking.

People who call themselves by their last names may be seen as exhibitionists, and referring to yourself by your first name makes one seem immature. Not only for business occasions, but in general, it is best to use *watashi*（私）when referring to yourself.

Calling someone's name without an honorific title is fairly intimate. Even at private occasions, it is basically best to refer to someone with a generic honorific title – *san*.

5

約束の時間の前に
到着するほうがよいのでしょうか？

日本人は、身だしなみを重要視します。外の風が強かったからといって、乱れた髪のままで相手に対面すると気遣いのない人と見なされるかもしれません。あるいは猛暑の日に汗をかいたままで相手に対面すると、無言のうちに暑さを相手に感じさせたり、清潔感のない人と思われることもあり得ます。

では、どのようにしたらよいのでしょう。答えは簡単、**約束の時間よりも早めに到着する**のです。日頃から汗かきの人は汗を静めるゆとりの時間を持つ。あるいは、化粧室で髪を整えることが必要かもしれません。

初めて行く場所や土地勘のない場所で駅から目的地までの時間が定かでない場合は、時間にゆとりを持ち、決して遅れることのないようにこころがけます。

早めに到着し、身だしなみを整えてもなお約束の時間よりも5分から10分程度早い場合、受付の手続きは済ませてもよいです。なぜなら、受付から会議室や応接室に案内されるまでの時間が必要となるからです（会社の受付や規模による）。

特に受付がなく、すぐに相手に会うことが予測できる場合は、相手が準備や別の業務をしている可能性があるため、**約束の時間ぴったりに伺う**ことがよいかと思います。早めに到着してしまったときは、周囲の人に迷惑がかからないところで時間の調整をしましょう。

Is it better to arrive early for an appointment?

Japanese people care about appearance. Even if the wind is blowing hard outside, if you have messy hair when you meet somebody, you may appear negligent. If you meet somebody while you are still sweating from the outside summer heat, you may bring the sense of heat into the room without intending to do so. Or, in the worst case, you may make the other person uncomfortable.

To avoid these situations, it is best to arrive early for your appointment. If you know you tend to perspire a lot, make sure you have enough time to cool down before the meeting. Or you may need to visit a rest room to comb your hair.

In addition, when visiting some place for the first time, you may not be familiar with the area or unsure of the approximate time required from the station. One should give enough time to be sure not to arrive late.

Once you arrive early and adjust your appearance, if you still have five to ten minutes before the appointment, you could check yourself in at reception. Depending on the size of a company, it may take some time to get to the meeting room.

In case there is no need to check in at reception and you are expecting to meet the person directly, it is best to wait till the time of your appointment, so you don't disturb the person if they are preparing for your meeting or taking care of another task. If you arrive early in these cases, be mindful that you don't cause inconvenience for others.

応接室、車内、電車内などで
どのあたりに座るのがよいのでしょうか？

応接室に通された後、席を指定されずに「しばらくお待ちくださ
い」といわれた場合、どの席に座って待つのかによってその人
の常識が測られることがあります。あるいは、部屋の奥の席に「どうぞ
お座りください」と案内されたからといって、すぐにその席に座ること
も望ましいとはいえないことがあります。なぜなら、**部屋の奥は上座**と
考えられているからです。

特に立場の高い方や年配の方などとお目にかかる場合は、すぐに
立って挨拶ができるよう、**出入り口近くに座る**こころ遣いが必要なこ
ともあるでしょう。

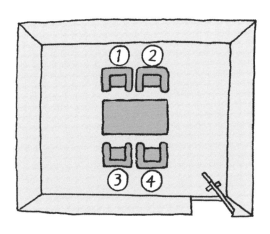

Where should I be seated in a meeting room, a car, or on the train?

When led to the meeting room and asked to wait without instructions about where to sit, your common sense may be tested. Even if they invite you to sit in the furthest seat from the door, it may not be wise to follow their suggestion, because the furthest seat from the door is considered to be the seat of honor.

In particular, when you are meeting someone with a high profile or an elderly person, you need to be seated near the door so that you can stand up and greet them as soon as they walk into the room.

車の中においては、タクシーやハイヤーなどは運転席の位置にかかわらず**後部座席の右側が一番**、左側が二番、中央が三番、助手席が四番です。相手の方が運転する場合は、その方を運転手さんのように扱わないという配慮から、**助手席が上席**と考えます。

　電車内では、**窓際が上座、通路側が下座**、三人がけは中央が最も下座、というのが基本です。ただし、化粧室に行きやすく携帯電話で話をするためにデッキにも出やすいことから通路側を好む方もいらっしゃいます。無理に上座をすすめるのではなく、相手の方の希望を伺い、そのお気持ちを優先する融通性も大切です。

自家用車

タクシー

In taxies or limousines, regardless of where the driver's seat is, the highest status is the right side of the back seat, followed by the left side of the backseat, the middle of the back seat and, finally the passenger's seat. In case the other person is driving, you should sit in the passenger's seat so that you are not treating the person like a driver.

On the train, in principal, the window seat is the seat of honor and the aisle is next. If it is a three-seater, the middle is the seat of least honor. However, some people prefer aisle seats since it is easier to access to the rest room and the deck for making phone calls. It is important to be mindful and accommodate their preference instead of giving them no choice but to sit in the seat of honor.

名刺の交換の仕方に決まりがあるのですか？

名刺の扱いで最も重要なことは、**名刺は単なる紙ではなく、相手の勤め先や名前などが記されている**ということを忘れずに取り扱う配慮です。

対面時はこちらから先に「○○と申します」と名刺を相手にお渡しし、挨拶することが基本ですが、上司に同行している場合は、上司から先に名刺交換をします。

What do I need to know about exchanging name cards?

The most important aspect about exchanging name cards is to remember when handling the card that it is not merely a piece of paper but has people's names and their company names printed on them.

It is recommended to be the first one to offer your name card when meeting someone. However, if you are accompanying your supervisor, let your supervisor go first.

自分の名刺は、角が折れていたり、少しでも汚れているものをお渡しすることは失礼です。このようなことがないように、外出する前には名刺入れのなかの名刺を確認します。

　相手と同時に名刺を交換する場合は、まず右手で自分の名刺を差し出し、相手の名刺を左手で受け取った後、すぐに右手も名刺に添え、丁寧に持って役職や名前などを確認します。お会いする方々が数人でそれぞれの方の名前を覚えられるときは、名刺入れに仕舞います。

　時折、片手で相手の名刺を受け取ったり、名刺をテーブルの上に置いたままで打ち合わせをしているうちにいつの間にか資料にまぎれてしまう光景を目にすることがあります。悪気がないことはわかりますが、前述の通り、相手の名前が記されているものを軽々に扱うことは、**相手を軽んじる行為に繋がります**。また、頂戴した名刺に、目の前で文字を書き込むことも失礼です。

Since sharing a name card that is bent or stained is unmannered, make sure to check the cards in your name card holder before heading out for meetings.

When exchanging each other's card at the same time, you should offer yours with your right hand and receive the other's with your left hand. As soon as your right hand is free, hold the person's card with both hands to show respect. Then confirm the printed information on the card such as the job title and name. If the number of people you exchange name cards with is small enough that you can remember their names, you can put the cards away in your card case.

Sometimes people receive name cards with one hand or leave them on the table during the meeting and end up losing them among hand-out materials. They may not mean to be disrespectful but, as mentioned before, carelessly handling something that has a person's name on it can make it appear that you are taking that person lightly. Writing a memo on someone's name card in front of that person is poor manners, as well.

仕事の関係者になぜ
おみやげを持参するのですか？

おみやげは持っていかなければならないものではありません。日頃お世話になっていることへの感謝をかたちにしたものがおみやげです。あるいは、初対面の方に対するものであれば、ご挨拶の気持ちとして持参することがあるでしょう。親しい仕事の関係者には、プライベートの旅行であっても、旅先のおみやげを差しあげることもあり得ます。おみやげは直接仕事に関係がないかもしれませんが、目には見えない時間を使っておみやげを準備することがこころの交流を深めるきっかけともなります。おみやげが会話の糸口になって場が和むこともあるでしょう。

また、依頼や相談、お詫び等で訪問する場合には、それぞれの状況における気持ちの表れとしておみやげを持参することもあります。

以前、パリで講演をした際、参加者から「日本人が仕事場にお菓子を持ってきてくれることがあるのですが、それにはどう対応したらよいのですか」と質問を受けたことがあります。その質問に対して「おもたせで恐縮ですが、といってそのお菓子を一緒に召し上がってはいかがですか」とお伝えいたしました。日本では相手から頂戴したおみやげをその方にすすめるときに「おもたせ（御持たせ物の略）」といいます。

このように、ときには仕事の関係者におみやげを持参することにも意味があるのです。

Why do Japanese people bring souvenirs to business partners?

It is not a written rule that you have to bring a souvenir. It is simply a way of showing your gratitude toward someone you associate with regularly. You could also bring a souvenir when greeting someone you meet for the first time. You might even bring a souvenir from a private trip for those with whom you have a close working relationship. Souvenirs may not appear to be directly related to your work, but the effort and care you take to prepare it might lead to a deeper interaction with your business associates. Talking about souvenirs is also a great icebreaker.

When you want to consult about or apologize for something, you can bring a souvenir as a representation of your state of mind.

Once after a lecture in Paris, a participant asked, "When a Japanese person brings a souvenir treat to work, what is expected of me?" My answer was she can open the package saying *Omotase de kyoshuku desuga* "Excuse me for opening your gift" and share the treat with them. In Japan, when you want to offer something to the person that brought the souvenir, you can use the word *omotase* "your gift".

As you can see, bringing souvenirs for business occasions can be a meaningful act when done properly.

本音と建て前、
どのように理解したらよいのでしょうか？

先方に仕事の提案をした際に「検討し、改めてご連絡差し上げます」といわれることがあるかもしれません。なぜその場で答えてくれないのでしょうか。

それは、これから先の人間関係を考えるからです。全く可能性がなくても、相手が不快な思いにならないよう、その場で直接的な表現で断ることを避けるのです。「前向きに考えます」といわれても、断られることがあります。対面している担当者がよいと思っても、上司に確認しなければ、提案を受け入れるか否かの判断ができないこともあるでしょう。

本音と建て前は、仕事にかぎったことではありません。「お食事をご一緒しませんか」と相手を誘ったとします。「出張が重なりしばらく難しい状況です」といわれた場合、本音はどこにあるのでしょうか。実際のところ返答がそれだけでは、本音は判断しにくいでしょう。そのほかに、補うことばが添えられているかどうかにもよります。

たとえば、自分が誘われた場合、仕事が忙しくてめどが立たないときであっても、**できるだけ誠意は伝えたいものです。**「来月下旬にはゆとりができます。誠に恐縮ですが、来月下旬以降でご一緒できましたら幸甚に存じます」などと、今は難しくても、その先の予定を具体的に知らせることで、先方にはお誘いに後ろ向きでない気持ちを理解いただけるでしょう。

How can I know one's *honne* "real intention" and *tatemae* "what one says on the surface"?

After pitching your idea to a business associate, you may be told "We will think about it and get in touch with you later." Why don't they tell you what they think right away?

That's because they value their relationship with you and even though they don't agree with your business idea, they prefer to avoid telling you so bluntly on the spot. Some may phrase it as "We will consider it positively" and still turn it down. There may be cases where even if the person you met likes your idea, he or she can't give you a definite response until they confer with their supervisor.

The concern about *honne* and *tatemae* occurs not just in business situations. Let's say you asked someone for lunch or dinner and that person replied, "It would be difficult for a while as I have several business trips coming up." What do you think the person's real intention is? In fact, you can't know for sure from this particular reply. It depends on how they follow up their comment.

When you are asked for lunch or dinner but are unfortunately too busy with work, it is best to at least communicate your intent sincerely. For instance, by being more concrete about your future availability such as "I will have more time by the end of next month. I would love to join you for a meal." In that way you can communicate that you are, in fact, interested.

Some may feel that it is a waste of time when Japanese people don't express their true intent right away, but I assume that sort of consideration to avoid hurting people's feelings does exist in other cultures as well. It's just that the Japanese way of wording it is much more subtle

その場で相手がすぐにはっきりと答えてくれないことをもどかしいと思う方がいらっしゃるかもしれません。しかし相手を 慮 るがゆえに本音をあからさまにいわないことは、日本人だけでなく外国人にもあり得るはずです。ただし、日本人の場合にはことばの選び方が細かく、間接的で繊細な表現のために、本音がわかりにくいのでしょう。

　日本人同士であっても、本音が掴めないこともあります。日頃から相手のことばの選び方、声のトーン、表情などから、その人のこころを読む。それを面倒がらずに、思いやりのひとつとして理解したいところころがけることが大切ではないかと思います。

and indirect so that it can make it harder to read one's real intention.

Sometimes it is difficult for a Japanese person to know what another Japanese person's real intention is. What's important is to understand the indirect expression is a way of Japanese delicacy. It is best to make an effort to read the other's intentions from their wording, tone of voice and facial expressions on a regular basis instead of thinking it's too much trouble.

訪問のアポイントメントを取る際に心得ておくべきことはありますか？その理由は？また、おいとまに関する心得は？

　特に仕事に関わる訪問は、アポイントメントを取る際にどの程度のお時間を頂戴したいのかをお伝えすることが相手への配慮といえましょう。なぜなら、相手が前後のご予定を調整しやすいからです。

　個人宅の場合も、親しい間柄でなくこちらから訪問依頼の連絡をする際には、その方の前後のご予定に支障をきたさないよう、同様の心得が必要です。また、個人宅への訪問は、食事の時間および食事の準備と片付けの時間を外すことが基本です。したがって、**午前の訪問は10時から11時、午後は2時から3時頃**が最も好ましいでしょう。11時の約束なら、相手の方が昼食の気遣いをなさらないよう、「30分ほどお時間を頂戴できますか」と長居しないことをさりげなく伝えます。夕方は夕食の買い物や準備が考えられるので、できるだけ避けましょう。

What should I know about making an appointment for a visit?
How about when I leave?

When making an appointment, it is thoughtful to let your hosts know how long you are expecting to stay, especially for business occasions. It would make it easier for them to plan their schedules.

Even when visiting private homes, if you are not yet that close with the people you intend to visit and you are the one who is contacting them for a visit, the same thing applies. You should also avoid mealtimes, including the time for cooking and clearing the table. Therefore, sometime between 10 am and 11 am in the morning or 2 pm and 3 pm in the afternoon are ideal times in the day. If you are going to visit someone at 11 am, it is a good idea to tell them you are thinking of staying for about 30 minutes, so that they don't have to worry about preparing you a lunch. It is best to avoid the evening so that you don't interfere with their dinner preparation.

つい話が盛り上がってしまい、予定よりも滞在時間が延びてしまうことがあるかもしれません。特に相手の方がその後に予定があるかどうかわからない場合、「ご多用のところ、長いお時間を頂戴いたしまして誠に申し訳なく存じます。そろそろおいとまいたします」と、相手の方のお気持ちを煩わせないこころ遣いが大切です。相手から「本日は貴重なお時間を頂戴いたしまして誠にありがとう存じます」「お時間は大丈夫でいらっしゃいますか」などと尋ねられた場合は、もしかすると相手の方のお時間に限りがあるのかもしれません。

　滞在時間に関しては、訪問する側、迎える側、双方に相手の事情を察する気持ちが重要です。

When you are having a good time, you may end up staying longer than expected. Remember to be mindful to make a comment that you are sorry for staying such a long time and you are thinking of leaving soon, especially if you don't know if the person has another appointment afterward. If the person tells you "Thank you for visiting me today" or asks if you are ok on time, there is a good chance that he or she has something that needs to be taken care of.

When it comes to the duration of the stay, it is important for both sides – host and guest – to be mindful and take hints from each other.

お宅訪問したときの
「なぜ」

Visiting Private Homes

相手の家には、
早めに到着してもよいのでしょうか？

相手宅の人は約束の時間までもてなしの準備をしてくださっている可能性があることを忘れてはいけません。約束の時間前に急な用件で外出していらっしゃることもあり得ます。したがって、たった数分であっても、約束の時間前に呼び鈴を鳴らすことは避けたいものです。

　約束の時間から5分以内をめどに到着することが最も好ましいかと思います。10分以上遅れてしまうと、道に迷っているのではないか、体調が悪くなったのではないかなどと心配なさるかもしれません。遅れることが早めにわかる場合、あるいは直前であっても、遅れる旨を電話、難しい場合はメールなどでお伝えしましょう。

　また、早めに到着してしまった場合、家の玄関やマンションの入口付近で待機していると、訪問を約束している方だけでなくご家族を含めて、出先から帰宅される際などに対面する可能性があります。したがって、入口から少し外れた辺りで過ごす配慮も忘れないでいただきたいと思います。

Is it OK to arrive at someone's house before the expected time?

You should be mindful that your host may be preparing for your visit until the last minute. It is possible that the host is out for an unexpected errand and won't be back until the time she or he is expecting you. Therefore, even if you are a few minutes early, you should avoid ringing the doorbell until the time you are expected to show up.

I think it is best to arrive no later than five-minute after the appointed time. If you are later than ten minutes, your host may start worrying whether you are lost or not feeling well. Once you know you are going to be late, even if it's at the last minute, it is thoughtful to let them know with a phone call, rather than an email if possible.

In case you arrive earlier than expected, be considerate to wait somewhere away from their front door, so that you won't run into the host or their family members coming back from their errands.

家に入る前にコートや帽子は
取りますか？

コートや帽子についていると考えられるものは何でしょう。その答えは、ちりや埃です。海外の方からすると、家に入る前からコートや防寒具類を取ることは失礼なのではないかとお思いになるかもしれませんが、**日本人は清浄感を保つことを重んじるがゆえ、そのようなものを室内に持ち込むことは失礼である**と考えます。

　一軒家の場合は、呼び鈴を鳴らす前にコートや帽子などを取ります。マンションであっても、エントランス手前で部屋番号を鳴らし、訪問者の姿が画面に映されるような場合は、コート類は取っておくことをおすすめいたします。

12

Should I take off my coat and hat before entering someone's home?

You can imagine that your coat and hat may be lightly covered in dust. From another cultural perspective, some may think taking off our coats beforehand would be impolite. However, as Japanese people highly value hygiene, bringing dust into someone's house is considered unmannered.

For a house, it is best to take off your coat and hat before ringing their doorbell. For an apartment, if they have a camera to buzz their guests in at the entrance, it is best to do so before you are on their video screen.

13

玄関で靴を脱ぐときは、
どうしたらよいのでしょうか？

　コートや帽子は埃のついたものと捉えるのですから、家に上がる前に靴を脱ぐことはいうまでもありません。したがって、自宅を出る前の身支度の段階で、靴下に穴は空いていないか、かかとの部分が薄くなっていないかなども確認しましょう。

　多くの人は、玄関に入って入り口の方向に向き直ってから靴を脱ぎます。つまり、帰る際にはそのまま靴を履くことができる方向で靴を脱ぐのですが、このようにすると玄関に入ってすぐに、出迎えてくださる方に背を向けることになってしまいます。

13

What do I need to know about taking off my shoes?

If you consider that coats and hats might be a bit dusty, it goes without saying that shoes would be even more so. People are expected to take their shoes off before entering someone's house in Japan. Therefore, you want to make sure, when getting ready for your visit, that there is no hole in your socks, or the heels of your socks are not wearing out.

Many Japanese people take off their shoes facing the door. That

したがって、玄関に入ったら、軽くご挨拶をし、**そのままの方向で靴を脱いでまずは上がりましょう。**その後、靴の方向に、斜めに向き直ってから、膝を床に着けて低い姿勢を取ります。お尻を後ろに突き出すようにしながら無理に手を伸ばして低いところにあるものを取る姿は安定に欠け、美しくないからです。

　次に靴の向きを直し、揃えて置きます。このときも出迎えの方に背を向けないようにこころがけます。揃えた靴は、中央を避けて下座側（出入り口に近い側、相手から遠い側）に揃えることで控えめな気持ちを表すことができます。

　また素足で外を歩いてきたときは清潔感に欠けるため、**素足のままでスリッパを履くことは好ましくありません。**特に汗をかきやすい夏の時期、サンダルで相手宅を訪問するようなときは、ハンドバッグのなかに靴下を携帯することをおすすめします。急な訪問でどうしても靴下を準備することができない場合は、お詫びを伝える配慮が大切です。

way, when you leave, you can put them back on without too much trouble. However, by doing so, you would end up turning your back to the host who came out to welcome you.

To avoid that from happening, it is best to take your shoes off in the same direction as you walked in and enter the house after greeting at the entrance. Then, you should turn sideways and put your knees on the floor to turn your shoes around. Reaching your shoes without kneeling and thrusting your buttocks back is not only unstable but also inelegant.

When turning your shoes around, be careful not to turn your back to the host and to align both shoes. By putting the aligned shoes closer to the door as well as further away from the host, avoiding the middle of the entrance, you can express your humility.

If you are not wearing socks, your feet may not be clean, so you should avoid wearing their slippers. Especially in the summertime, when you are wearing sandals to someone's house, it is best to carry a pair of clean socks in your bag. In case you visit someone unexpectedly and are not able to bring your socks, you can at least be mindful to share a small apology.

14

おみやげには、
どのようなものを準備したらよいですか？
おみやげを渡すとき、
なぜ「つまらないものですが」というのでしょう？
紙袋のままで渡してよいですか？

おみやげは、相手に対するこころをかたちにしたものです。たとえば、高級な果物をたくさん持って伺うことによって相手の気持ちの負担になってしまうようなら、そのおみやげは活かされてはいないわけです。訪問先の家族の人数、年齢、嗜好などを日頃の会話から理解しておくことは、おみやげを購入するときに役立ちます。親しい間柄でない場合、基本的には食べ物やお酒など、後に残らないものがよいでしょう。

購入時の注意点として、訪問先近くのお店での購入は避けます。なぜなら、間際までおみやげを準備していなかった印象を与えかねないからです。

おみやげを渡すとき、へりくだりの気持ちから「つまらないものですが」という日本人が多いよう

14

What should I bring as a souvenir?
Why do Japanese people say *Tsumaranai mono desuga* "It's nothing special but I hope you like it" when handing over souvenirs?
Should I give a souvenir with or without the paper bag?

A souvenir is a way of expressing your feeling toward the other person. For instance, if bringing many expensive fruits becomes an emotional burden to the host, that isn't the best choice. Knowing the number of family members of the host, their ages and tastes from daily conversation can help in selecting an appropriate souvenir. If you don't know the person so well, in principle, it is best to bring food or drinks, something that doesn't last long.

You should avoid purchasing from stores close to the place you are visiting. It could give an impression that you didn't try to prepare until the last minute.

It is true that many Japanese people say *Tsumaranai mono desuga* as a way to stay humble. Being humble is a good thing, but I personally think it is not necessary to say *tsumaranai* "nothing special." Instead, you can say *Kokoro bakari no mono desuga* "It's a small gift for you." This way, you can communicate a sense of respect and self-restraint at the same time.

How about a paper bag? What is a paper bag for? It is for the guest to keep the souvenir neat and clean during transportation. And just like your coat, since it is likely be carrying a bit of dust, you should avoid handing your gift in the paper bag. After handing over the sou-

に感じます。謙遜するのは悪いことではないですが、あえて「つまらないもの」という表現をしなくてもよいのではないかと思うのです。かわりに**「こころばかりのものですが」**と伝えると、相手を重んじながら慎みのこころも表現できます。

さて、紙袋は何のためにあるのでしょうか。持参する人が道中、品物を汚さずに、しかも持ちやすいこともあって、紙袋を使用するわけです。コートと同様に紙袋は埃^{ほこり}がついていると捉えるため、そのまま差し上げることは控えます。**紙袋からおみやげを出してお渡しした後、紙袋は持ち帰る**ことが基本です。先方が「紙袋をお預かりいたしましょうか」といってくださる場合は、すぐにお願いするのではなく、一、二度は遠慮し、それでも預かるといってくださるときには素直なこころで「恐れ入ります」とお願いいたします。

遠慮することや、どうぞと譲ることが行き過ぎてしまうと、互いのストレスになりかねません。これを**「三辞三譲<ruby>三辞三譲<rt>さんじさんじょう</rt></ruby>」**といいますが、辞退も譲ることも三度以上にならないようにいたしましょう。

venir, you are expected to bring the paper bag home with you. If your host offers to take it from you, you should first turn it down once or twice, but if the host still insists, you can ask them to do so by saying *Osore irimasu* "Very much appreciated."

Being too modest or too passive can create an awkward moment. In Japan, turning down or offering a favor up to three times is a virtue but be mindful not to do more than three times.

座る場所に決まりがあるのですか？

ビジネスの場と同様にご自宅を訪問するときも、**和洋室ともに部屋の奥を上座とする**ことが基本です。和室には床の間がありますが、この床の間の近くの席を上座とするのが和室の特徴といえましょう。

なぜ床の間が上座なのか。それは、床の間の起源説のひとつからもひもとくことができます。床の間のもととされる押板と呼ばれる場所には、僧家の影響によって仏画を掛けて三具足（香炉、燭台、花瓶）を飾り、礼拝することが多かったといわれています。つまり、床の間は神

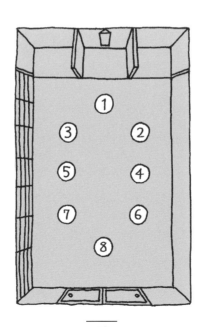

15

Where should I be seated?

Similar to business occasions, basically, the furthest seat from the door is the seat of honor in one's house whether it's a Japanese style or western style room. When a Japanese style room has an alcove "*tokonoma*", the closest to the alcove is the seat of honor.

The reason why the alcove defines the seat of honor has something to do with its origin. As a part of Buddhist ritual, many people used to hang Buddhistpaintings and place incense burners, a candle holder and a vase in the alcove for worship. The alcove is considered to be sacred.

Some also say the raised rooms of the nobility were the basis for the alcove. Either way, the alcove is associated with a sense of honor and

聖な場所ということです。

　また、高貴な人が座る場所を上段の間といい、その場所が床の間に変化したという説もあります。いずれの説によっても、床の間が高位の席であることは確かです。したがって床の間の近くは、上司、年配者など、その場において重んじられるべき人が座すところであり、自ら進んでその位置に座ることは望ましくありません。**特に若い世代の方は、出入り口付近の席に座るようにこころがける**とよいかと思います。

　また、おみやげの項（56頁）で触れた三辞三譲の精神は席次に関しても必要です。高位の席であっても、相手や周囲の方が何度かすすめてくださる際は、控えめなこころで、感謝のことばを伝えてからその場所に座る融通性も忘れないようにいたしましょう。

higher social status. That is why seniors, your supervisors or someone who is important in the room should be seated near the alcove and you should not be willing to take your seat there. It is best especially for young people to sit near the door.

The above mentioned three-time rule applies to seating as well. When you are offered a seat of honor, if the host offers you several times, you should be mindful to accommodate their favor and communicate your gratitude, then be seated with modesty.

16

正座は足が痛くて無理。
どうしても正座しなくてはだめですか？
楽に正座する方法はありますか？

武士は、敵に襲われたときにもすぐに立つことができるようにと、あぐらや片膝を立てた状態で座ることが基本でしたが、江戸時代になって平穏な生活へ移り変わると、正座が浸透していきました。なぜなら**正座は、主人の尊厳を保ちながら服従心や相手に対して敵意がないことを示す姿勢**であるからです。このように考えると、正座はしびれることがあって当たり前の座り方ともいえましょう。また正座が中心となった背景には、畳の普及も大きな影響があったと考えられます。

　さて、男性はズボンで足が圧迫されやすいこともあり、正座が苦手な方が多いのではないかと思います。改まった場では正座が好ましいとは思いますが、無理はよくありません。正座が苦手な方は、ご挨拶のときだけは正座になり、そのほかはあぐらでもよいでしょう。ただし、自分が使うスペースが広がらないように、他者から見て不快な座り方にならないようにとこころがけることは忘れてはなりません。

　次のポイントを基本に、正しい姿勢で座りましょう。

Seiza "sitting on one's knees" is painful. Is it unavoidable? Is there a trick to make it any easier?

Samurai used to sit with their legs crossed or raising one knee so that they could stand up quickly when their enemies attacked, but as it became more peaceful in the Edo period, *seiza*, the style of sitting on one's knees became pervasive, because sitting in *seiza*, not being able to swiftly rise up, shows a sense of one's surrender and lack of intention to behave with hostility. Learning its origins, you know that it's meant to be physically difficult and it is not a surprise that your legs grow numb. It is also possible that the fact that *tatami* "reed mats" became a popular flooring material in people's houses has influenced the way Japanese people sit.

That said, I hear many men don't do well with *seiza*, possibly because wearing trousers compresses their legs more. It is ideal to sit in *seiza* at formal occasions, but nobody should be forced to do so. If you are not good at *seiza*, it is acceptable to start with *seiza* when greeting and cross your legs afterward, but be mindful not to use too much space or to make others uncomfortable.

《正座のポイント》

・かかとに全体重が乗らないように。

・上体が前方に傾かないように腰を沈める。

・女性は両膝を合わせ、男性はひとこぶし分ほど空ける。

・足の親指同士を3、4センチほど重ねる。

・両手は指を揃えてハの字に腿(もも)の上に置く。

・顎(あご)を引く。

しびれたときは、**跪座(きざ)という姿勢をとり、しびれを取る**ことをおすすめいたします。跪座は、立っている状態から正座になる、正座の状態から立つ、いずれもこの姿勢を経由します。また低い姿勢で動作をする際にも基本となる姿勢です。

《跪座》

・正座の状態から少し腰を浮かせ、片足ずつつま先を立てる。

・左右のつま先、かかとを離さないように。

・左右のかかとをあわせた真上に腰を落ち着け、後ろに反(そ)り返らないように、上体を上方に伸ばすような気持ちで座る。

《How to sit in *seiza* properly》
· Do not rest all of your weight on your heels.
· Sit down straight so that your upper body doesn't lean forward.
· Women should sit with their knees together and men should leave the space of a fist between them.
· Cross your big toes over each other about 1 to 1.5 inches.
· Place both hands in your lap in a triangle shape with your fingers closed.
· Draw your chin in slightly.

When your legs start feeling numb, you can try to sit in *kiza* to manage the numbness. *Kiza* is the position you go through when sitting down to or standing up from *seiza*. It is also the basic posture when you want to do something from a lower position.

《How to sit in *kiza*》
· From *seiza* lift your hips up enough to accommodate resting the balls of your feet on the floor.
· Make sure your toes and heels are not too far apart.
· You should then lower your buttocks directly onto both heels ensuring you do not lean backwards. You should feel your body stretching upwards.

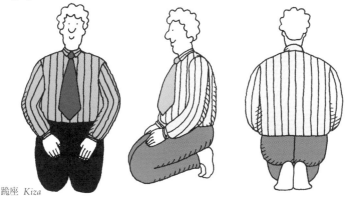

跪座 *Kiza*

旅館や和食店での

「なぜ」

Visiting
Ryokan and Japanese Restaurants

17

床の間に関する
決まりごとはありますか?

前にも触れましたが、**床の間は仏画を掛け、三具足を置いたこ**とからもわかるように神聖な場所として扱われてきた背景があります。ゆえに現代においても床の間に座ることはいたしません。基本的に足で踏むことも失礼です。なぜなら、神様がいらっしゃる場所をむげに踏みつけることは避けるべきだからです。

　理由はそれだけではありません。床の間には掛軸が掛けられ、香炉や花が飾られることがあります。床の間のしつらえにはもてなす側のお客様に対するこころが込められているのです。悪気はなくても、**床の間に自分の荷物を置いてしまう、飾られているものを勝手に移動させるなどは、準備してくださった方のこころを軽んじている**と取られてもしかたありません。

　さて、一般的に厳格な和室は、床の間のほかに、床の間の横には僧侶の書見の場所である付け書院（書院）と、二枚の棚板を段違いに取り付けた違い棚などの床脇が

あることを理解しておくとよいでしょう。正面奥の左に床の間、その左側に書院、右

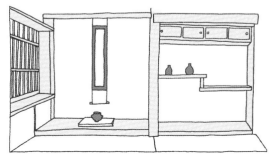

What is the alcove and what do I need to know about it?

As mentioned in chapter 15, the alcove *"tokonoma"* is where people used to hang Buddhist paintings and place Buddhist objects. It is considered to be sacred and for that reason, you should never sit in an alcove, even now. You should also avoid stepping on the alcove as much as possible, as you should treat the place where Japanese gods reside with respect.

There is another reason why we should treat the alcove with care. To this day, people hang scroll paintings or place incense burners and flowers in the alcove. The alcove display is the representation of the host's hospitality to their guests. Thus, even if you don't mean it, if you put your luggage on the alcove or move the ornaments for some reason, it would be interpreted as you are taking their hospitality lightly.

A more formal Japanese room will be furnished with a *shoin* "a study, where monks used to read" and a *tokowaki* "a space where staggered shelves are installed" next to the alcove. When the alcove is on the left side of the room, the accompanying *shoin* is on the left and the shelves on the right, this style is called *hon-gatte*. When the shelves are on the left side of the alcove and the *shoin* on the right, the style is called *gyaku-gatte*.

Let's explore more about the three Buddhist objects – the incense burner, candle holder and vase. The proper way of displaying these objects in the *tokonoma* are, the incense burner in the middle, the candle holder on the right and the vase on the left. Sometimes people use five objects including two candle holders and two vases. In this case place the incense burner in the middle with one candle holder on each side

側に違い棚があるつくりを「本勝手」と呼びます。床の間の左に違い棚、右に書院があるつくりは「逆勝手」と呼びます。

　香炉、燭台、花瓶の三具足について、さらに深めてご説明いたします。香炉を中央、その向かって右側に燭台、左側に花瓶を置きます。ちなみに五具足といって燭台と花瓶が二つずつの場合は、中央に香炉、香炉の左右に燭台、さらにその外側左右に花瓶を置きます。

　香炉は、お香を焚くために必要な道具ですが、単に香りを楽しむためだけでなく、場を清浄にするためのものでもあります。

　燭台はろうそくを立てる台ですが、ろうそくの火は、穢れを祓う浄化の作用があるともいわれています。香に関する心得とともに、燭台の扱い方について、燭台に三本の足がある場合は二本を正面として取り扱うなどと

いう教えが小笠原流礼法の古文書に記されています。

　三つ目は花瓶（花立て）です。花をいけることで信仰心のみならず、感謝の念や季節を表現することができます。

　さて床脇の違い棚には、香炉、香箱、硯箱、筆、料紙（文字を書く紙）などを置きます。書院は僧侶が勉強するための出窓が起源ともいわれ、硯、筆、墨、筆架などの文具を置きます。

　このように、和室は単に畳を敷き詰めただけの部屋ではないことがおわかりいただけたのではないかと思います。ひとつひとつの飾りに気づくことができると、さらに楽しみが増え、こころの交流にも繋がるのではないでしょうか。

of it and a vase on either side of the candle holders.

The incense burner is used not only to enjoy the aroma from the burning incense, but also to purify the space.

The flame from a candle is also believed to carry a purifying effect. Ogasawraryu-reihou's old documents mention manners regarding incense, as well as how to handle the candle holder, such as when there are three legs attached to it, you should face two legs to the front.

This brings us to the vase. By offering flowers one expresses not only faith but also shows gratitude and seasonal awareness.

The staggered shelves hold the incense burner, incense container, inkstone and box, with brushes and writing papers. As it is originally believed that the *shoin* was a bay window where monks used to study, people place writing objects such as an inkstone, brushes, ink and a brush holder in the *shoin*.

As you can see, Japanese style rooms offer much more than just *tatami*. Once you learn about these objects, you can appreciate the space more and really enjoy the hospitality of the host.

18

和室でしてはいけない ことはありますか?

和室と洋室の大きな違いは出入口のつくりです。洋室には頑丈なドアがあり、鍵がかかりますが、和室には襖はあるものの、ドアに比べると容易に壊すことができ、何よりも鍵がありません。お互いの信頼とこころ遣いによって、お互いの尊厳が保たれ、襖はドアの役割をはたしてきたわけです。現代において、特に旅館等では襖の手前に戸を設けて鉤を取り付けているところが多いですが、数十年前までは家の玄関も鍵をかけていなかったという話を地方の方に伺ったことがあります。

　ドアがない分、中にいる人のプライバシーは、襖の開け閉ての作法によって守られます。

　まず、襖は勢いよく一度で開けることはいたしません。

①

What are some taboo behaviors in Japanese style rooms?

Unlike western style rooms, Japanese style rooms do not have a solid door that can be locked. Instead, the rooms are divided by *fusuma* "sliding doors". They are a much simpler build and usually don't have locks. By mutual trust, compassion and maintaining each other's dignity allows the *fusuma* to play the role of a door. These days some people are putting locks on their *fusuma*, especially *ryokan* "Japanese inns" but I have heard that until a few decades ago people in the countryside didn't even lock their homes!

As the *fusuma* are not locked there are manners to be observed when opening and closing them to honor the privacy of the people inside.

You should avoid opening a *fusuma* in one movement. It is best to be done in three steps. First, you sit in *seiza* in front of the *fusuma* and open about two inches using the handle (1). This gives the people a sign that you are about to enter the room. Depending on the situation, you may announce your entrance by saying *shit-*

襖の開閉は三回に分けて行うことが基本です。襖手前で正座をしてから、襖の取手に手をかけて五、六センチほど開けます（①）。これが「室内に入ります」の合図にもなります。状況によっては、その前に「失礼いたします」などと声をかけます。

　次に、取手から襖の端に手を移して、さらに下に移動させ、身体の中心あたりまで襖を開けます（②）。これにより部屋の中の状況を確認することができ、中にいる人は身づくろいするなど、互いに顔を合わせる前に相手を受け入れるこころ構えができるわけです。

　今度は反対の手に替えて、身体が通れる程度まで襖を開けます（③）。このとき、襖を開けにくいようならば、少し身体を襖の側に向けると開けやすいでしょう。

　部屋に入るには、正座から立って入る場合と、正座のまま、膝行（手を身体の脇について進むこと）で入る場合があります。大事なのは、**敷居を足で踏まないこと**です。

　敷居は建具ですので、足で踏むと建物そのものに影響を与える可能性があります。しかも敷居は簡単に替えられるものではありません。また、敷居はその家を象徴するものとも捉えられ、敷居を足で踏むことはその家の人への敬意に欠けるとも考えられていました。「敷居は親の頭、だから踏んではいけない」といわれることもあります。

　敷居とともに、踏まないほうがよいものが畳の縁です。「**畳の縁を踏んではいけない**」とお聞きになったことがあるかもしれませんが、これにも理由があります。

　まず、武家においては畳の縁に繧繝縁、高麗縁など格の高いものが用いられたことに由来します。このように厚みのある縁を用いると、畳と縁に少々の段差が生まれます。お膳などを運ぶ際には、段差を考慮して歩かないと縁に足を躓かせて周囲に危険を与えかねません。

surei shimasu "excuse me" beforehand.

Next, slide your hand down the edge of the *fusuma* from the handle and open it to the center of your body (2). Now you will be able to see what's happening in the room and it gives

time for the person inside to get ready before officially greeting you.

Next change your hand and slide the door open enough to show you to enter (3). If it's hard to open, moving your body closer to the *fusuma* can make it easier.

When entering the room, you can either walk in by standing up from *seiza* position or enter in *seiza*, moving forward by using your arms and sliding on your knees. In either case, it is very important not to step on the threshold.

The threshold is the joined sill frame of the entrance and stepping on it may cause damage to it. In addition to the fact it's not easy to replace, people used to think that the threshold represents the house itself and stepping on it shows your lack of respect to the house owner. Some even say, "the threshold is like the head of your parent."

Another thing you should avoid is stepping on the borders of the *tatami*.

It comes from the tradition that *samurai* families used to use high quality edging on their *tatami*. The special materials created a thickness to the edges causing them to stand out so if you were not careful when bringing food in on trays, you might trip posing danger to others.

There is also the notion that the border of the *tatami* represents

畳の縁を境界線と心得ることも大切です。畳の縁によって、心理的な領域が保たれることにもなります。相手の前にある縁を越えることで、それまで保たれていた好ましいお互いの距離感が縮まりすぎてしまい、相手に心理的な圧迫感を与えてしまうとも考えられます。

　敷居、畳の縁は、できるだけ踏まないようにこころがけましょう。

one's emotional or psychological borders. Stepping over the closest *tatami* border to a person may break the favorable psychological distance between you and that person and give a sense of pressure to that person.

It is best to be mindful not to step on the threshold and the borders of the *tatami* .

和食の席で心得ておくことはありますか？

食事の席で**清潔感を重んじる**ことはいうまでもありません。おしぼりは食事が始まる前に手を清潔にするために提供されるものですが、このおしぼりで顔や身体を拭くことは、同席者に不快感を与えるだけでなく、お店の方にも失礼です。

洋食と同様に、**すするなどの音は避けたい**ことのひとつです。そばを食べるときはすすってよい、といわれることが多いですが、あらたまった席では、そばであっても音は慎むことが好ましいのです。

舌鼓や、お茶などで歯をすすぐ音も嫌われます。無意識に行っていることがあるかもしれないので、ご自身でしていないかどうかを意識することも大切です。

そのほかの音への配慮として、日本料理は器を手に持ちますので、**器を置くときは音を立てないように静かに置きましょう**。

日本料理は、四季に応じた旬の食材を用いて、細やかに季節を表現する工夫がされています。たとえば、春には食材が桜色に染められ、夏には涼やかにガラスの器が用いられ、秋には紅葉が添えられ、冬には椿の葉に餅粉で雪を表現するなど、さりげなく自然が表現されています。目には見えないところで時間をかけて準備されたお料理は、食材の命をいただくことを含めて、**感謝しながら食べるこころ持ちが食事作法の根本**です。「**いただきます**」といってから食事を始める習慣は、こうした気持ちの表れといえましょう。素材そのものの味を楽し

What do I need to know about dining at Japanese restaurants?

It is good manners to set great value in cleanliness when dining. Wet towels are for cleaning your hands before eating. Using them to wipe your face or body is unmannered to your company at the table as well as to the restaurant staff.

Just like dining in western restaurants, you should avoid making eating noises such as slurping. You may have heard that *soba* is an exception in Japan, but when you are at formal restaurants, you should avoid making any noises even while eating *soba*.

The sound of chewing and rinsing your mouth with tea should be avoided, too. People often make these sounds unconsciously. It is important to be conscious of whether you do or not.

You can hold dishes and plates while eating Japanese food, but it is important to avoid making jarring noises when placing the dishes back on the table.

Japanese food incorporates the four seasons into its cooking and representations. In spring, some ingredients are dyed in cherry blossom colors. In summer, glass vessels are used to add a sense of coolness. In fall, autumn leaves may be used to decorate the dish. In winter, rice cake flour may be added on a camelia leaf to represent snow. These visual effects are meant to be subtle but take extra effort and time to prepare. To appreciate such dedication, in addition to the fact you are going to consume the lives of your ingredients, the fundamental manner of eating Japanese food is to appreciate what is being offered. Japanese people say *itadaki masu* "we shall receive" before dining. It is a good representation of that spirit. It is also a characteristic of Japanese

むことも日本料理の特徴といえます。

　食事をする側に欠かせない心得は、**美しい所作で感謝を表現する**ことです。最近、肘をテーブルについたまま食事をする方を多く見かけますが、同席者に不快感を与えるだけでなく、お料理を作ってくださった方や食材に対しても失礼です。猫背の前屈みで食事をすることは、犬食いといって昔から嫌われています。

food that you enjoy the flavor and freshness of the ingredient itself.

Another fundamental matter in eating Japanese food is to express your appreciation of food through your manners. Placing your elbow on the table is not only disturbing to your company, but also disrespectful to those who cooked the dishes as well as toward the lives of the ingredients. Hunching over while eating is called *inu gui* "eating like a dog" in Japan and should be avoided.

箸の持ち方や箸の素材に
決まりはありますか？

　日本のほかにも箸を用いる国はありますが、スプーン等を用いずに箸のみで食事をするのは日本くらいでしょう。食材をつまむ、切る、ちぎる、割くなどすべての動作を箸のみで行うわけです。

　食事の作法は「箸に始まり箸に終わる」といわれるほど、箸遣いは大切です。小笠原流には「箸先五分長くて一寸」という教えがあります。箸先の汚れは一・五センチから三センチ以内に止めよ、いうことです。なぜなら、それ以上箸が汚れると、他者へ不快感を与えかねないからです。

　まず、箸の正しい持ち方を身につけましょう。どのような持ち方でも食事はできる、というお声もあるかとは思いますが、箸を正しく持つことで、食べ物を取り上げるだけでなく、割く、ちぎるなどの細かな動きがしやすくなります。

　箸遣いを直したい方は、自分に合う長さの箸を選ぶと使いやすいでしょう。親指と人差し指を直角に広げ、両方の指先を結んだ長さの一・五倍がちょうどよい長さといわれています。

　正しい持ち方は次の通りです。

①上の箸を人差し指と中指ではさみ、親指を添えます。

　下の箸を、親指と人差し指の股部分と薬指で支えます。

②親指を軸にして、上の箸のみを動かします。

What do I need to know about chopsticks?

There are other cultures that use chopsticks to eat, but Japan is probably the only country not using spoons or other secondary utensils. You are expected to pick, cut, tear and take apart all the ingredients with your chopsticks.

There is a Japanese saying, eating manners begins with chopsticks and ends with chopsticks. Ogasawara school teaches that you should only be using up to one inch from the tip of your chopsticks when eating, because any more than that may make others uncomfortable.

First, you should be able to hold your chopsticks properly. Some may feel it doesn't matter as long as you can eat, but holding chopsticks properly allow you not just to eat but to tear and take apart the ingredients easily.

It is best to choose chopsticks that are the right length for you. It is said that the appropriate length is to double the length from the tip of your thumb and index finger when opening them to 90 degrees.

《How to hold chopsticks properly》
1　Hold the upper chopstick with between your index finger and middle finger, then press down gently with your thumb.
　　Hold the lower chopstick in the web of your thumb pushing it down gently against your ring finger.
2　Move only the upper chopstick using your thumb as support.
　　Try to hold them about two-thirds from the tip.

Chopsticks come in different grades. The highest grade is *yanagi*

持つ位置は、箸先から三分の二程度のところを目安にします。

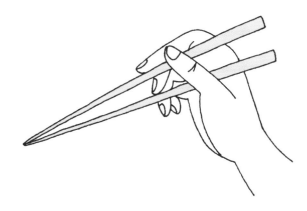

　さて、箸にも格があります。最も格の高い箸は、正月などに一度かぎりで用いられる柳箸（やなぎばし）です。なぜ格が高いかといえば、箸は神様の依（よ）り代（しろ）であり、神人共食（しんじんきょうしょく）の大切な道具、つまり神聖なものですので、**本来は使い回しをせずに一度かぎりであることが求められる**からです。したがって、高価なものでも、塗りや銀製などの箸は、再使用しない割り箸よりも格が低いのです。自然環境保全が叫ばれる昨今ではありますが、基本的な思想として、ここにも日本人の清浄観が感じられるのではないかと思います。

bashi which is used for New Years and meant to be used only once. Chopsticks are considered to be an object by which the Japanese gods are summoned and a sacred means for humans to dine with divine spirits. That is why, primarily, chopsticks are not meant to be used multiple times and why disposable chopsticks are higher grade than other expensive lacquer or silver chopsticks. The idea may not go so well with today's environmental movement, but you can see how the Japanese fundamentally value cleanliness even in the custom of using chopsticks.

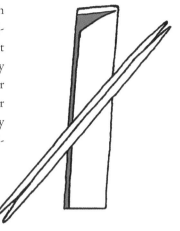

柳箸 *Yanagi bashi*

21

避けたほうがよい箸遣いについて、教えてください。

箸に関する作法は、正しく持てるだけでは十分ではありません。次に上げる「**嫌い箸**」と呼ばれる箸遣いも避けるようにこころがけてください。

《嫌い箸》

・寄せ箸：箸で器を引き寄せる

・涙箸（なみだばし）：箸先から汁を垂らす

寄せ箸 *yose bashi*

・刺し箸：食べ物に箸を刺して口に運ぶ

・指し箸：人や物を箸で指し示す

涙箸 *namida bashi*

・探り箸：料理の中身を探るように箸を動かす

・迷い箸：どれから食べようかと箸を宙に迷わせる

迷い箸 *mayoi bashi*

Are there any taboos related to the use of chopsticks?

In addition to holding your chopsticks properly, it is best to avoid using chopsticks as listed below.

《Breach of chopstick manners》
· *yose bashi*: Drawing a dish toward yourself with your chopsticks.

· *namida bashi*: Dripping liquid from the tip of your chopsticks.

· *sashi bashi* (with 刺): Skewering food with your chopsticks in order to pick it up.

· *sashi bashi* (with 指): Pointing toward someone or something with your chopsticks.

· *saguri bashi*: Using your chopsticks to find a food you like by rummaging in dishes and pots.

· *mayoi bashi*: Hovering your chopsticks back and forth over side dishes, when trying to choose which one to take.

· *oshitsuke bashi*: Pressing food such as rice in the bowl before eating.

· *watashi bashi*: Resting your chopsticks across the top of your dish.

· *hiroi bashi*: Passing food from one person's chopsticks to another's.

・押しつけ箸：ご飯などを器のなかで
押し固めて口に運ぶ

・渡し箸：箸を器の上に渡して置く

・渡し箸（拾い箸）：はさんだ食べ物を
箸から箸へ渡す

・ねぶり箸：箸先をなめる

・移り箸：一度箸をつけたものを食べ
ずにほかの料理へ箸を移す

・にぎり箸：箸をにぎったまま片手で
器を取り上げる

・諸起こし：箸と器を同時に取り上げ
る

　なお、ご飯に箸を刺して立てること
は立箸（仏箸）といって、亡くなった方
に供える枕飯を連想させるので避け
ましょう。

押しつけ箸 *oshitsuke bashi*

渡し箸 *watashi bashi*

- *neburi bashi*: Licking your chopsticks.

- *utsuri bashi*: Jumping your chopsticks from side dish to side dish without eating.

- *nigiri bashi*: Holding a dish or bowl while you are holding your chopsticks.

- *moro-okoshi*: Holding your chopsticks and a dish or bowl at the same time.

Another even more serious taboo of chopstick manners would be stabbing chopsticks vertically in a bowl of rice. This is reminiscent of the *makura-meshi* "pillow of rice" offering used at funerals for the deceased. It should be avoided as it would be considered ill mannered and is said to bring bad luck.

- *Tate bashi* "standing chopsticks"
- *Hotoke bashi* "Buddha chopsticks"

食事中、とくに注意すべきことは、
ほかにありますか？

小笠原流の伝書に「貴人を見合わせて喰うべし」とあるように、同席者のなかで最も高位な方や年長者のペースに合わせて食事をするこころ遣いも大切です。たとえば、改まった席では高位の方が箸を取るまでは食事を始めません。高位な方が箸を置いて食事を終えた場合、その他の人はできるだけ早く食事を終えるこころがけが必要です。

さて、汁が垂れそうなときや料理がこぼれそうなとき、箸を持っていない側の手のひらを受け皿のようにすることも避けたい所作のひとつです。おしぼりで手を清めてはいますが、手で受けたものをいただくことは同席者に不快感を与えます。代わりに椀の蓋や懐紙を受け皿として使用してよいのですが、それ以前に、一口大にした食べ物をあせらずに口に運ぶよう、日常の食事から気をつけていただきたいと思います。涙箸（86頁）にならないためにも、しょうゆ皿や煮物の入った器など、大きな器や皿でなければ基本的に手で取り上げてよいのです。

ひとつの器に何種類かの料理が盛ってある場合、自分の食べたいものから好き勝手に食べることも、探り箸と同様に品格を損ないます。薄い味のものから濃い味のものへと移ると、それぞれの味わいを楽しめます。たとえばお刺身は、手前に白身魚やイカ、奥にマグロなどが盛りつけられていますので、基本は手前のものから奥のものへと

What do I need to know while I am dining at a Japanese restaurant?

According to the Book of Ogasawara, you should eat in conformity to the people of high standing. Therefore, it is important to dine at the pace of those who are of higher social status or are the elders of your group. For instance, in a formal setting, you should not start eating till the person of higher status picks up their chopsticks. Once the person finishes his or her meal, be mindful to finish yours as soon as you can.

When soup or sauce is about to drip from your chopsticks, you should avoid trying to catch it with your hand. Though you did clean your hands with a wet towel using them like that may make others uncomfortable. Instead, you can use a bowl lid or *kaishi* paper, but it is always best to cut your food into bite-size pieces and bring it to your mouth without rushing. In order to avoid *namida bashi* (p.87), it is acceptable to hold a dish of *shoyu* or simmered food up when enjoying Japanese cuisine, as long as they are not too big.

When there are several dishes placed on one plate, eating only from the one you like is considered as unmannered as *saguri bashi*. Starting from plain flavored dishes and moving to rich flavored dishes is a good way to enjoy each distinctly different flavor. For instance, *sashimi* plates often place white fish and squid in the front and tuna in the back. You can basically eat from the front to the back.

You don't need to eat fish skin if it's not your favorite but if you leave any part of the food on the plate including fish bones or a fruit pit, it is best to put them together in the corner of the plate so they will not be too visible to the others.

食べ進みます。

　魚の皮は、苦手であれば無理に食べなくてもよいのですが、魚の骨や果物のたねなどを含めて何か**料理の一部を残すときには、同席者の目に立たないように皿のすみにまとめておきましょう**。

　料理を食べ終えたときに、片付けやすいであろうという好意であっても、**皿や器を重ねて置くことは好ましくありません**。特に塗り物と磁器や陶器を重ねてしまうと、漆や蒔絵を傷める可能性があります。

　かまぼこやいかの天ぷらなど、**箸で切れないものは歯でかみ切る**しかありません。しかし、かみ切った後に歯形を残したままの食べかけのものをお皿に戻すことは、見苦しいので控えます。ではどうしたらよいかというと、**くっきりと歯形が残らないように、一口食べた後、すぐに右端と左端を食べ、できるだけ切り口がまっすぐになる**ようにこころがけます。

　割り箸を割るときは、同席者に箸が近づかないように、**箸を自分の側に引き寄せた位置で、横ではなく縦に割ります**。

　器を受け取ってすぐに食べることを「受け食い」といい、卑しい印象として嫌われます。受けた器は**一度テーブルや折敷の上に置きましょう**。

When you are done eating, even if you mean well to help clearing the plates and dishes, you should not place them on top of each other, because you may damage the coating especially by putting lacquered bowls and pottery or porcelain vessels together.

Certain food such as *kamaboko* "minced and steamed fish" or squid *tempura* leaves you no choice but to bite them off instead of cutting them with your chopsticks. However, you should avoid putting the half-eaten piece of food which has your teeth marks back on the plate. It is unappetizing to look at and in order to avoid this, you can try to eat them in two bites, the right half and left half, so that it won't leave obvious teeth marks and makes a somewhat straight line.

When splitting your disposable chopsticks, keep them away from your company and draw them close to you, then split vertically instead of horizontally.

Eating food off of the plate as soon as you receive it is called *uke gui* and it is considered to be unmannered. You should place the dish you receive on the table or the tray first, before appreciating it.

23

箸を休めるときは どうすればよいですか?

食事の手を休めるとき、ナイフやフォークをテーブルではなくお皿にかけるように、**箸は膳の縁(ふち)にかける、または箸置きに置きます**。膳の縁にかけるときは、**汚れた部分が膳の左外側に出るようにし**、箸置きがある場合は膳の中に置きます。

料理店だけでなく、**一般家庭でも箸置きを用います**。なぜ器の上に箸を置かないかというと、前述の通り「嫌い箸」と呼ばれるもののひとつに「渡し箸」(箸渡しとも、88頁)があり、器にお箸をかけることを嫌うからです。三途の川(亡くなって七日目に渡るとされる川)を連想させる、あるいは食事が終わったことを表すゆえ、渡し箸は好ましくないといわれています。特に、**箸先を対面する人に向けて置くことは、大変失礼**なことと心得ましょう。

What do I need to know when I want to put down my chopsticks?

When you want to take a pause from dining, you can rest your knife and fork on the plate but you should place your chopsticks over the edge of your tray or on your chopstick holder. If placing over the edge of the tray, make sure to leave the tips of your chopstick outward toward the left. And place the chopsticks on the tray when there is a chopstick holder.

People use chopstick holders in private residences, too, not just restaurants, in order to avoid *watashi bashi* (p.87). Placing your chopsticks over a plate or bowl is also poor manners since it is associated with the Sanzu River, which the souls of the deceased must cross before reaching the afterlife. Also, it implies you are finished with your meal in Japan. It is also important to remember that placing your chopsticks so that the tips are pointing at someone is considered to be extremely rude.

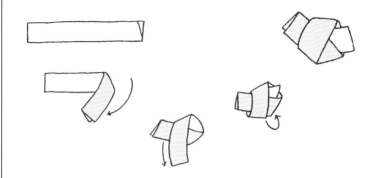

　箸置きはなくても箸袋があれば代用できます。**箸袋を千代結びに して、箸置きの代わりに**します。

　ちなみに、左利きの方は、危険を防ぐということからも、箸置きの位置などは動かしてもかまいません。

　膳、箸置き、箸袋もないときは、器の端にかけるしかありませんが、そのような場合でも、できるかぎり同席者に不快感を与えないようにとの気遣いが大切です。やむをえず渡し箸をするときは、せめて器の手前上に置きましょう。このような時は、箸が下に落ちないように注意するとともに、他者の目に立たないようにします。

　また話が弾むと、気づかないうちに箸を持ったまま話し続けてしまうことがあるかもしれません。このようなことがないよう、まず箸置きに箸を置くことをこころがけましょう。

When you don't have a chopstick holder, you can use the chopstick wrapper as an alternative. You can fold it up to create a makeshift holder for your chopsticks. If you are lefthanded, it is acceptable to rearrange your chopstick holder in order to avoid accidents.

When you have neither a chopstick holder or chopstick wrapper on your tray, you may have to set your chopsticks on a plate or bowl. In this case it is important to be mindful not to make others uncomfortable. Be careful to not allow the chopsticks to roll over and drop, and when you set them down do so as discreetly as possible.

When you are having a good time, sometimes you find yourself talking while you are still holding your chopsticks. It is best to avoid that from happening and be mindful to place your chopsticks down while chatting.

24

椀の蓋の扱い方を
教えてください。

椀の蓋を開けるときは、蓋の内側についているしずくを外にこぼさないように気をつけなければなりません。次の手順で開けると、粗相なく安全に蓋を開けられます。

《蓋の開け方》

①左手で器を押さえながら、蓋の糸底を持つ

②手前から向こう側に開ける

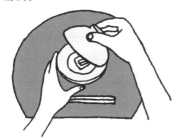

③さらに椀にそって半円を描くように
回してしずくを切る

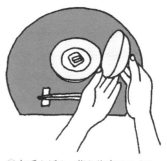

④左手を添え、蓋を仰向けにする

What do I need to know to handle a bowl lid?

It is important not to spill the condensed water inside your bowl lid when opening it. Here is a safe way to open your lid properly.

《How to open the bowl lid》
1 Hold the bowl with your left hand then take the top of the lid with your right hand.

2 Open the lid from the front and tip it away from your body.

3 Turn the lid in a half-circle along the edge of the bowl to drain it.

4 Then using both hands turn the lid over.

5 Set the lid on the outside of your tray with both hands.

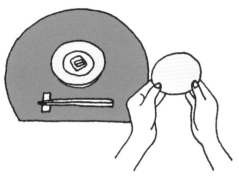

⑤蓋を膳の外側に両手で置く

　蓋が開けにくいときは、椀の縁を左手または両手でたわめて開けやすくします。

　蓋を閉めるときは、逆の手順で行いましょう。蓋は運ばれてきたときの状態に戻しますが、しずくを切らなくてよいので、半円を描く必要はありません。

《蓋の閉め方》
①両手で蓋を取り、右手で蓋の糸底を持つ
②蓋を椀の向こう側につけてから、手前に向かって閉める
③椀と蓋がおちつくようにして合わせる

　左利きの方は、蓋の開閉についても、左手を中心に行ってかまいません。

When it is hard to open, you can flex the edge of the bowl with your left hand or with both hands to assist in sliding the lid off.

To put the lid back on the bowl, you can follow the steps in reverse. The idea is to return the bowl back to how it was when it was brought to you. But naturally, since you don't need to drain the lid this time, you do not need to turn it in a half-circle.

《How to close the bowl lid》
1   Hold the lid up with both hands and hold the top of the lid with your right hand.

2   Align the lid touching the edge of the far side of the bowl and tip it toward the front.

3   Set the lid on top of the bowl.

*If you are lefthanded, you can reverse your hands.

お酒を酌み交わすときの
決まりはありますか？

ワインは注がれている間、グラスに手を触れることはありませんが、日本酒は手に取った盃に注ぎます。武家社会において、男性は左手、女性は右手を主に盃を持つことが基本でした。理由のひとつとして、武士はすぐに刀を抜けるようにと利き手を空けていることが求められたからです。しかし、現代であればそのような心得は必要ありませんので、粗相がないように利き手を主に盃を持つことが望ましいかと思います。

　盃の持ち方は、糸底の高い盃は人差し指と中指で糸底をはさみ、親指を添えます。

　女性は右手で盃を持ち、左手を底に添えます。

　平たい盃は、両手で下から支えるように持ちます。

　お酒を注ぐときにも、作法があります。当たり前のことですが、注ぐ量を加減しないと、盃からお酒がこぼれてしまいます。そこで、前半は少なめ、中ほどは多め、後半は少なめの量を注ぐようにします。この注ぎ方を小笠原流では「鼠尾、馬尾、鼠尾」と呼びます。

　お酒を注ぐとき、酒器や瓶は両手で扱い、粗相がないように注意します。相手が飲みにくくないよう、お酒はなみなみとは注がないようにいたしましょう。

What do I need to know about drinking manners?

You do not hold your wine glass up when wine is poured. However, in Japan, you are expected to hold up your *sake* cup when *sake* is poured. During the time of the *samurai*, men would hold the cups in their left hands and women would hold them in their right. It is said that the *samurai* would hold it in this way to accommodate drawing their sword quickly if challenged. There is no need to follow such customs any longer and in order to avoid any spills, it is best to hold your cup with your dominant hand.

The proper way to hold a *sake* cup with a taller foot is to take the rim between your index finger and middle finger and place your thumb on the side of the cup.

A woman is expected to hold her cup with her right hand and place her left hand on the bottom of the cup.

For a shallower cup, you can raise the cup with both hands propping it up at the bottom.

It is not too surprising that if you are not careful when pouring *sake* into a cup, it might spill. There is a particular manner of pouring *sake* in order to avoid that from happening. Start by trickling in a little, then increase the flow and at the end ease off. In the Ogasawara tradition this method of pouring is called "*sobi, babi, sobi*" referring to a mouse's tail, a horse's tail and mouse's tail.

Remember to use both hands to handle *sake* cups and bottles when you are pouring in order to avoid spilling. Also, try not to pour too much *sake* in the cup as it will make it harder for the other person

乾杯の際は、目の高さに押しいただきます。相手からお酒をさされた際も同様にいたします。

　ところで、日本では「盃をいただく」「お流れを頂戴する」と表現することがあります。神様からいただいたお酒を、同じ盃を用いて一同が飲むことで絆や結束力を強化したいと考えたのでしょう。清浄を重んじる日本人が同じ盃で飲むところから、その思いが深いことが推測できるのではないでしょうか。

to drink.

For a toast, it is best to hold your cup at eye level. You can do the same when you are offered a drink.

In Japan, people say "we receive a cup of *sake*" or "let's share a cup of *sake*". It is a remnant of the tradition that, when people used to drink *sake*, they felt they were receiving it from the gods and drinking from the same cup would enhance their bond. Knowing how much the Japanese value cleanliness you can see how significant the gesture of drinking from the same cup is.

26

抹茶を飲むときに
茶椀を回さないといけないのはなぜですか？

抹茶を飲む際、二回ほどに分けて茶椀を回します。その理由は、正面を避けるためです。

茶椀は、もてなしてくださる側がお客様のために選んだものです。こころを込めて準備して点(た)てた抹茶が入っている茶椀が、正面を向けて置かれていることを軽んじてはいけません。抹茶を飲むときには、慎(つつし)みのこころで受けることが大切なので、茶椀の正面に口をつけることがないようにと茶椀を回すわけです。

茶椀は時計回り、反時計回りと、流派によって回す方向が異なりますが、最も大切な心得は、謙虚なこころで抹茶を頂戴することなのです。

飲み終えた後、高い位置で持ちながら茶椀を拝見することは危険で失礼です。できるだけ低い高さで、茶椀を落とさないようにと気遣いながら両手で丁寧に扱いましょう。

Why do I need to turn the tea bowl when drinking *matcha*?

When you are drinking *matcha*, you are expected to turn the bowl twice before drinking. This is to avoid drinking from the front of the bowl.

The host chooses an appropriate bowl for their guest and makes your tea with the greatest care. You cannot take their hospitality, placing the front of the bowl toward you, lightly. It is important that you receive it with a humble attitude.

The direction in which to turn the bowl depends on the principles of the various tea schools, but the most important aspect is to accept the bowl of tea with a sense of humility.

When looking at the bowl after drinking do not elevate it too far from the ground, this could be considered dangerous and a bit rude. You should view the bowl in the lowest possible position and handle it with both hands to avoid dropping it.

大浴場での決まりを
教えてください。

大浴場にかぎらず、公共の場でのふるまいは、周囲の人への思いやりが重要です。何度も記してきましたが、清潔さを欠かさないようにする配慮を忘れないようにしましょう。

　まず、髪が長い人はゴムやヘアーキャップなどを用いて、浴槽のお湯に髪の毛がつからないようにします。このようにすることで、髪の毛が床に落ちることも防げます。

　衣服は、脱衣室にあるかごやロッカーに畳んで入れます。タオルで身体の前面を軽く覆って浴室へと向かうことは、女子の嗜み（たしな）です。

　浴槽に入る前に軽く身体を洗い流します。立ったままシャワーを浴びたり、桶でお湯を身体にかけると周囲にお湯が飛ぶことがあるので注意します。

　浴槽に入る前は、かけ湯をして身体をお湯に慣らせます。かけたお湯が浴槽に入らないようにしましょう。タオルをお湯につけると不衛生なので、浴槽の外に置きます。

What do I need to know
about public baths?

When you are in a public space in Japan, not just at a pubic bath but in general, it is especially important to be mindful of others. The sense of cleanliness is the key aspect.

If you have long hair, make sure to tie it up or cover it with a hair cap, so your hair will not soak in the bath water. By doing so, you also prevent your hair from falling to the floor.

You can fold your clothes and place them in the basket or locker in the dressing room. It is best for women to cover the front of their body with a small towel.

Make sure to wash yourself quickly before going into the bathtub. It is important to be careful not to splash people near you by standing up to shower or pouring water over your body too aggressively.

Before entering the bath, you should pour hot water from it over your shoulders using a bucket to get used to the temperature. Be mindful not to splash that water back into the bath. You should not bring your towel into the bath as it is considered unsanitary. You can

身体や髪を洗った後、使用したボディーソープやシャンプー類は元の位置に戻します。桶や椅子も同様です。

　浴場を出る前は次に使う人のことを考えて、髪の毛や泡が残っていないかどうかを確認します。また、濡れたままではなくタオルで拭いてから脱衣室に向かいましょう。

　脱衣室内のドライヤーで髪を乾かしたときは、洗面台に落ちた髪の毛をティッシュペーパーで取って捨てます。この心得は、大浴場だけでなく、日常生活で洗面台を用いるときにも欠かせません。

　また、大浴場はこどもの遊び場ではないのです。こどもを連れて大浴場に行く場合、大きな声で騒がないことも大切ですが、特に浴槽を長時間占領してしまうことがないように心得ましょう。最後まで、他の人のことを考えながら行動していただきたいと思います。

keep it outside of the bath.

After washing your hair and body, make sure to return the shampoo and conditioner to where it was. The same for your bucket and small chair.

When leaving the bath, be mindful to see if you didn't leave any hair or soap bubbles in the tub. Be sure to dry yourself with your towel before walking into the dressing room.

If you use a hair dryer in the dressing room, make sure to clean up any hair that have fallen into the sink with a tissue paper. This is something that can be practiced not just at public baths but in our daily life as well.

In case you accompany children to a public bath, remember that it is not a playground. Refrain from making too much noise, and also be careful not to occupy the bathtub for too long. Again, the key is to stay mindful of others.

日本ではチップは必要ないと聞いたけれど、
「こころづけ」とは何ですか？

　日本にはチップがない代わりに、料理店や宿泊施設の料金にはサービス料が加えられていることがあります。一方、日本では昔から、こころづけというものが活用されてきました。

　こころづけは、特別な配慮に対する感謝のしるしとして渡すものです。チップとこころづけの大きな違いは、チップはサービスを受けた後に渡し、こころづけはサービスやお世話を受ける前に渡すことといわれます。また、こころづけはお金を小さな袋に入れる、または紙に包みます。なぜなら、お金を包まずに渡すことは、相手に失礼であると考えるからです。包む過程が相手へのこころ遣いを表します。日本人は直接的よりも間接的な表現を好むのです。

　さて、私が幼い頃、祖母が常に小さな和紙の袋にお金を入れたものを準備して、新幹線のホームに荷物を取りに来て車まで運んでくださるポーターの方々、宿泊先のホテルで荷物やルームサービスを運んでくださる方に渡していたことを記憶しています。つまり、サービスを受ける前だけでなく、サービスを受けた後にも、お世話になった感謝のしるしを差し上げる習慣が日本にないわけではありません。

　旅館では、部屋に自分が宿泊する部屋の係りの人が挨拶にきたタイミングで、「これからお世話になりますが、よろしくお願いいたします」という気持ちを込めて、こころづけを渡します。最近は、サービス料がついているのでこころづけを受け取らない、またはチェックアウト

I hear people don't tip in Japan.
What is *kokoro zuke?*

You don't have to tip in Japan. Instead, some restaurants and hotels include a service charge in their fees. But also, Japanese people have traditionally practiced the custom of *kokoro zuke* (gratuity).

Kokoro zuke is a way to represent your gratitude for service. The difference between *kokoro zuke* and tipping in western culture is you offer *kokoro zuke* before you receive a service instead of after. Also, you should put your *kokoro zuke* in a small paper pouch or wrap it up with paper. Handing unwrapped money is considered rude in Japan. The act of wrapping expresses your appreciation for that person. Japanese people favor indirect expressions to direct ones.

That said, I remember my grandmother used to prepare small envelopes made of Japanese *washi* paper with money in them and handed them out to our porters at train stations and hotels. So, it does not strictly have to be before to show your gratitude for a service.

At *ryokan*, it is best to hand a *kokoro zuke* when your waitress visits your room for the first time. Recently, some *ryokan* have decided not to accept *kokoro zuke* since they include their service charge in the fee. Some places hand you a receipt for your *kokoro zuke* when you check out. The proper amount of *kokoro zuke* is said to be 10 to 20% of your room charge, but *kokoro zuke* should not feel mandatory. The most important aspect of *kokoro zuke* is that you would voluntarily like to offer a gratitude to someone who takes care of you well.

の際にこころづけにも領収証を渡してくださる旅館があります。こころ
づけの金額は宿泊料の1、2割程度が目安といわれますが、大切なこ
とは「渡さなければならない」ではなく、自発的に「差し上げたい」とい
うこころの存在です。

　そのほか、結婚披露宴やパーティーの受付などでお世話になる
方々に「こころづけ」として、封筒（金封）やぽち袋などに紙幣を入れ
て感謝の気持ちとして渡すこともあります。

Another type of *kokoro zuke* is when you hand it out to those who help you with the reception at a wedding or parties. You can place money in an envelope or small paper pouch as a representation of your gratitude for them.

冠婚葬祭の
「なぜ」

Ceremonial Occasions

「冠婚葬祭」って何ですか？
とくに「冠」がわかりにくいので教えてください。

冠は加冠、すなわち成年式を表しており、こどもの成長に伴う儀礼です。婚は婚礼、葬は葬式、祭は葬式に続く先祖供養の祭祀です。

現代において冠は成年式だけでなく人生の通過儀礼、祭は年中行事を指すことが一般的です。ここでは冠についてご説明いたします。

こどもの成長に関するお祝いをいくつかご紹介します。まずは妊娠五カ月目の戌の日に腹帯を巻いて祝う「帯祝い」、そして「出産祝い」。生後七日目にこどもに名前をつけて健やかな成長を願う「お七夜」。男児は生後三十日から三十二日目、女児は三十一日から三十三日目に土地の守り神となる産土神に誕生を報告し、氏子として認めてもらい無病息災を願う「お宮参り」。百日または百二十日目に初めて食事をさせる儀式「お食い初め」。初めての誕生日を祝う「初誕生」。そして初めて迎える「初節供」、「七五三」(P.166)、「成人式」などがあります。

次に「長寿祝い」があります。平均寿命が延び、昨今は六十歳の還暦祝いが長寿のお祝いとしてのイメージと結びつかなくなっているのではないかと思います。還暦だけは満年齢、その他の長寿祝いは数えの年齢でお祝いすることが多いでしょう。

還暦は十干十二支が一巡し、暦が生まれた年に還ること。赤は厄を祓い、また赤ちゃんに還るということから、赤い頭巾やちゃんちゃん

What does *kan-kon-so-sai* "ceremonial occasions" mean in Japan?

*K*an (冠) represents the coming of age and it refers to the ritual occasions in which people celebrate children's healthy growth. *Kon* (婚) means weddings, *so* (葬) indicates funerals and *sai* (祭) symbolizes other memorial services for one's ancestors.

Today, *kan* (冠) means not only the Coming of Age Day for 20 year olds, but also includes other initiation rituals, and *sai* (祭) represents all the annual events in Japan. This section introduces rituals that celebrate healthy growth related to *kan* (冠).

On the day of the dog at five months in pregnancy, an expectant mother wraps a *haraobi* maternity belt around her waist to recognize the healthy growth of a baby. Once delivered, they celebrate the baby's birth. At seven days old, people pray for better growth by naming their babies – *oshichi-ya*. Boys visit shrines at 30 to 32 days old and girls at 31 to 33 days old to inform the *ubusuna-gami* god of their birth and to pray for their protection and sound health – *omiya mairi*. Eating real food for the first time is a weaning ceremony – *okui-zome*. The first birthday is *hatsu tanjo*. First *sekku* is called *hatsu zekku*, followed by other ceremonies including *shichi-go-san* (p.167) and *seijin shiki* "coming of age ceremony".

Later in life, Japanese people celebrate their longevity. Now that the average life expectancy has increased, celebrating 60 years old may not feel so relevant but celebrating a 60th birthday in real age and every other ten-year birthday in calendar years is commonly practiced.

kanreki: Celebrating the 60th birthday as the ten stems and the twelve signs of the Chinese zodiac complete the cycle and one's cal-

こが贈られます。

　古稀は七十歳の祝いで、昔は七十歳まで生きることが稀であったことによります。

　喜寿は七十七歳の祝いで、喜の略字が「㐂」であることによります。

　傘寿は八十歳の祝いで、傘の略字「仐」が八十と読めることによります。

　米寿は八十八歳の祝いで、米の字が八十八に分けられることによります。

　卒寿は九十歳の祝いで、卒の略字が「卆」であることによります。

　白寿は九十九歳の祝いで、百の字から一を取ると白になることによります。

　その後は、百歳を百賀、さらに百一賀、百二賀というように、毎年祝います。

　長寿祝いではありませんが、厄落としという風習があります。数え年で男性は二十五歳、四十二歳、六十一歳。女性は十九歳、三十三歳、三十七歳が一般的な厄年ですが、地域により異なる場合もあります。男性四十二歳と女性三十三歳を大厄、厄年の前の年を前厄、後の年を後厄と呼びます。お気づきの方がいらっしゃるかと思いますが、数え六十一歳の厄年は、還暦の祝いと同じ年に迎えます。厄年には悪いイメージがあるかもしれませんが、同時に人生における節目の年齢を迎えたことを示し、だからこそ心身ともに浄化して物忌み（一定期間食事や行動を慎み, 不浄を避け, 家内にこもること）をする必要があったわけです。大厄の男性四十二歳、女性の三十三歳は仕事や子育てが忙しく、体調を崩しやすい時期でもありまうす。厄年は、健康管理に留意することを考えるよい機会と捉えてはいかがでしょうか。

endar goes back to their birth at the age of 60. Since the color red exorcises evil spirits and puns with baby in Japanese, people often send a red hood or red padded *kimono* jacket as a gift.

koki: Celebrating the 70th birthday as it was rare to live till 70 years old in old times.

kiju: Celebrating the 77th birthday as the simplified *kanji* character for *ki* (喜) consists of three sevens (㐂).

sanju: Celebrating the 80th birthday as the simplified *kanji* character for *kasa* (伞) can be read as 80 in Japanese.

beiju: Celebrating the 88th birthday, the *kanji* character for *bei* (米) consists of 88 in Japanese.

sotsuju:Celebrating the 90th birthday, the simplified *kanji* character for *sotsu* (卆) can be read as 90 in Japanese.

hakuju: Celebrating the 99th birthday as removing one (一) from the *kanji* character for hundred (百) becomes white (白), which can be read *haku* in Japanese.

People celebrate every year after the 99th birthday. *Hyaku-ga* for 100, *hyaku-ichi-ga* for 101, *hyaku-ni-ga* for 102 and so on.

In addition to celebrating longevity, there is also the *yaku-doshi* ritual for exorcism and driving bad luck away. Critical years for men are generally 25, 42 and 61 years old. Women are 19, 33 and 37 years old, but it can vary depending on regions. 42 years old for men and 33 years old for women is considered to be most critical year in a person's life and the year before, *mae-yaku*, and after, *ato-yaku*, are also part of the ritual. I'm sure some of you may have noticed that the 61st *yaku-doshi* year will be the same year as the 60th year *kanreki* birthday celebration. Marking the stages of one's life, people used to drive bad luck away and purify their bodies and souls by fasting and staying home to avoid the unclean. Even today, 42 years old for men and 33 years old for women are the times in life when people are busy with work and raising children. You may be more vulnerable to becoming sick. The *yaku-doshi* ritual can be an occasion to look after your health.

日本の結婚式の
決まりごとを教えてください。

最近は割愛されることが増えてきましたが、本来は結婚の前に結納があります。「結」は血縁結社を表します。平安時代は男性が女性の血縁に入れてもらうことを主としましたが、武士が活躍する時代になると女性が男性の家に嫁ぐ形式に変わっていきました。つまり、日本における結婚の形式は婿入り婚から始まり、武士の勢力が高まると嫁が実家から輿や馬で婿方へ向かい、婿の家で夫婦固めの式が行われる嫁入り婚へ変化したわけです。神前結婚式が広まるまでは、家庭で結婚式が行われることが主流でした。

日本には婚約に伴う契約書がありませんが、一般的に結納を行うことが婚約成立を意味します。現代では結婚式と披露宴のときにのみ仲人を立てることがありますが、元来は結婚する男性と女性を生涯にわたって指導するという立場の介添えの人（身分の高い男女）が必要とされました。介添人であり結婚に関する保証人、それが仲人なのです。しかしながら、結婚は家と家の結びつき、という概念が薄らぐにつれて、昨今は結納の代わりに、両家の顔合わせとして食事の席を設けるのみで結婚式を迎える傾向にあるようです。

さて、日本には神式、仏式、キリスト教式などの結婚式があります。なぜ信者ではないのに日本人は教会で結婚式を挙げるのだろうか、と思う方がいらっしゃるかもしれません。その理由を簡単に述べることは難しいですが、理由のひとつとして、日本には八百万の神が存在

What do I need to know about Japanese weddings?

More young couples skip this ritual today but traditionally *yuino*, a "betrothal gift" takes place before the wedding. *Yui* (結) means the bonding of blood relatives and, in the Heian period, it meant the groom joining the bride's family. While that was the original custom, as *samurai* gained power, it switched to the bride joining the groom's family. The brides would ride in a carriage or on a horse from her parents' to the groom's house where their wedding would be held and she would became a member of his family. Until Shinto-style weddings became popular, it was common to hold a wedding at one's home.

There is no contract exchanged in Japanese weddings, but generally holding a *yuino* is what makes your engagement official. Today, marrying couples tend to ask their matchmaker to only attend their wedding and reception party. However, traditionally matchmakers were a man and woman of high status and their role was to supervise the couple throughout their marriage. They were primary caretakers and guarantors for the marriage. That said, the idea of marriage being the unification of two families has become less relevant and lately couples tend to hold their weddings after a family get together introducing both families to each other instead of hosting a *yuino*.

Japanese people hold their weddings at a shrine, temple or church. Some may wonder why mostly non-Christian Japanese like to have weddings at churches. One of the reasons is that Japanese people believe in many gods. Having a historically agricultural background, Japanese have been coexistent with nature and thought the gods reside in everything surrounding us. That worship for nature met with Shinto-

するとされていたことが挙げられます。前にも記しましたが、日本人は農耕民族であったゆえ、常に自然と共存し、生活を取り囲むあらゆるものに神が宿ると考えていました。その自然崇拝が神道と結びついて、八百万の神といわれるような多神教になりました。先祖あるいは血縁という集団の守護神である氏神、住んでいる地域や都市の産土神が日本人の信仰の土台にあるのではないかと思います。そのことからも「無宗教」の日本人は多いですが、「無神論」ではないため、クリスマスを受け入れ、教会での結婚式にも抵抗がないと推察できます。

またファッションの面から、ウエディングドレスで結婚式を挙げることへの憧れで教会を選ぶとの理由も否めません。

さて、神前結婚式は、大正天皇（当時は皇太子）の御婚儀が御神前で行われたことを記念して日比谷神宮（現在の東京大神宮）が始めたのが最初といわれています。

小笠原流には結婚の儀が伝わっていますが、現在とは異なり、結

ism and formed Japanese polytheism. *Uji-gami* is the guardian god for your ancestors and blood relatives. *Ubusuna-gami* is the guardian god for the place and area you live in. Among many other gods, these two gods are the foundation of Japanese belief. Many Japanese people are non-religious, but it doesn't mean they are atheist. That may explain how Japanese people enjoy celebrating Christmas and are open to the idea of having weddings at churches.

There is also an aspect of fashion. Many brides like to wear wedding dresses and choose church weddings.

It is said the origin of Shinto-style weddings at shrines goes back to the wedding of Emperor Taisho, who was a prince at that time, in 1900.

In the Ogasawara tradition, a wedding takes place over several days. First, the groom and bride wear white *kimono* and both drink nine cups of *sake* in white earthenware cups in a nod to their marriage-vows at an *in-no-shiki* "ceremony of yin". Then a *yo-no-shiki* "ceremony of yang" takes place three days later with colored *kimono* and red earthenware cups. This may be the origin of the custom of brides and grooms changing their dress at wedding receptions today. Exchanging marriage vows is performed with a minimal group of people including the groom, bride, bridesmaid and two people who serve *sake* in the cups. Not even parents are included. And it is later that family members share *sake* as a recognition of becoming an extended family and relatives. It is nice to be celebrated by your family and friends, but this simple approach of exchanging marriage-vows calls to mind today's weddings.

婚に関する式は一日で終わるものではありません。まず「陰の式」。白の着物で式三献（三々九度）があり、男女ともに白土器で九盃ずつお酒を飲み、夫婦固めの盃が交わされます。その三日後に色物の着物で赤土器を用いる、現在のお色直しともいえる「陽の式」が行われました。婚礼儀式の中心である夫婦固めの盃は、新郎と新婦、花嫁の介添人、酌にあたる二人と極めて少ない人数で両親さえ出席することなく行われ、その後に親子固めの盃、親類固めの盃などが席を改めて行われていたのです。ゲストに祝福していただくことも大切ですが、新郎新婦二人の誓い合いを感じさせる簡素な結婚式のあり方は、現代にも通じる部分があるのではないでしょうか。

　ところで、結婚式に関してではないのですが、小笠原流の伝書に「迎え小袖の心得」というものがあります。迎え小袖とは、新郎の側が新婦を温かい気持ちで迎える証として、新郎の家紋をつけ、新婦に合わせて仕立てた着物を贈ることを指します。当時新婦は、顔も見たことがない新郎のもとに嫁ぐ状況が珍しくなかったのですから、新婦の心情を思うとこのような配慮がどれほど重要であったかを察することができます。この「迎え小袖」のあり方、着物にかぎらず、取り入れることができる、素敵な思いやりのかたちではないかと思います。

Not directly related to the wedding ceremony, but according to the Book of Ogasawara, the groom's family used to tailor *kimono* with their family crest for the bride. This gift embodied their warm welcome to the bride who was coming to marry the groom whom she had never met before. It was not uncommon in old days. It must have eased her anxiety a great deal. This way of showing compassion to someone is something we can adopt not necessarily with *kimono* but with other items even today.

31

結婚祝いに関する心得を教えてください。また、披露宴に伺う際、気をつけることはありますか?

結婚祝いに関しては、「切れる・別れる・割れる」といったことを連想させるガラス、陶器、ナイフ、包丁、はさみ、鏡などは避けるべきとされていました。しかし、昨今はペアのワイングラスやカップなどが贈られることも少なくないようです。事前に結婚祝いの品を送る場合は、結婚式の一カ月前をめどに、少なくとも一週間以上のゆとりをもって相手宅に到着するようにいたしましょう。

また実際は結婚祝いの品物ではなく、披露宴当日に金子包み(祝儀袋)を持参することが多いのではないかと思います。その際、新札を準備するのも祝う側のこころの表れです。お祝いに限らず、紙幣を差し上げるときには必ず新札を包むようにいたしましょう。また、金子包みの裏側の上下の重ね方は、まず上から下に向けて折ってから、下から上に被せます。これにより「喜びごとが天を向く」「喜びごとを受け止める」ことを示すなどといわれます。

金子包みはハンドバッグやジャケットの内ポケットに直接入れるのではなく、帛紗に包んで持参します。紫の帛紗は慶弔に両用できますので、まずは一枚、準備しておくと便利です。受付前に到着したら、帛紗から金子包みを出し、「本日はおめでとう存じます」とことばを添えて渡します。

31

What do I need to know about a wedding gift or when attending reception parties?

It used to be considered bad luck to send objects that can be associated with cutting, separating or breaking such as glassware, earthenware, knives, cooking tools, scissors and mirrors. However, it is no longer so much of a taboo to send a pair of wine glasses these days. If you are sending your gift before the wedding, it is best to send it one month before the ceremony. At the latest, one week prior.

That said, most people bring gifts of money in an envelope on the reception day. Presenting new bills is a way to display your congratulatory feeling. Not just for celebratory occasions, but whenever you hand bills as a gift, it is best to prepare new bills. To prepare the back of the envelope, fold the top of the envelop downward first and fold the bottom upward covering the first fold. People believe the folds represent a sense of upholding the celebration.

The envelope should be wrapped and carried in *fukusa* "silk cloth" and not in your handbag. Purple silk cloth can be used for both congratulatory and condolatory occasions. When arriving at the reception desk, open the silk cloth and hand over the envelope with a word of congratulations.

結婚式や披露宴に伺う際の装いは、新郎や新婦と同色のものを着用しない、すなわち白を避けるのはもちろんのこと、お色直しの色を事前に伺うことができれば同色を用いないようにこころがけます。またあくまで主役は新郎新婦ですので、目立つ装いやお化粧は避けます。

　自分本位にならず、状況を考えて身だしなみを整え、行動することが出席する側の責任ともいえましょう。

As a guest at reception parties, you should avoid wearing the same color of clothes as the bride and groom, which is white. If you have a way of knowing the color of their second dress, it is best to avoid that color as well. Also, it is important to remember the center of attention should be the marrying couple and you should not stand out too much with your clothing or make-up.

It is the etiquette of the guests to dress and behave in a manner that is respectful and deferential to the marrying couple.

日本の葬式について教えてください。
通夜と告別式とは違うのですか。

　日本ではかつて土葬が中心でしたが、西暦700年に法相宗の開祖・道昭が火葬されたことが始まりで、その数年後に持統天皇の火葬が行われたともいわれています。その後も土葬は根強く残っていましたが、大正時代以降は火葬が普及し、現代ではほぼ100パーセントが火葬です。

　通夜は本来、近親者だけで行うものでした。その日の夜は、ひとつの布団で亡くなった人と一晩寝ることがならわしでした。なぜなら、死はけがれとされていたため、死者とこもることで、そのけがれを他者に及ぼさないようにとの考えからです。しかし、現代では近親者だけでなく、友人、知人なども通夜に出向くようになったのは、死をけがれとはとらえなくなったことの表れです。むしろ、故人との別れを惜しみ、遺族の方々を慰めるこころが強くなったともいえましょう。

　このように、通夜に伺う人は、故人と親しい間柄にあったということです。「お通夜と告別式、どちらかに伺えばよいですか」との相談を受けることがありますが、故人と親しい間柄であった方は、通夜と告別式のいずれにも出席することが基本です。ただし、仕事の都合などで告別式に伺えないなどというときは、このかぎりではありません。

What do I need to know about Japanese funerals? What is the difference between a wake and funeral?

Historically burial was common in Japan, but after monk Dosho who played an influential role in the founding of Buddhism in Japan was cremated in 700, it is said that Emperor Jito was also cremated a few years later. Burial was dominant even after that, but cremation became more popular in the Taisho period (1912 – 1926) and now almost everyone in Japan is cremated.

Originally, only close relatives attended a wake. It was a custom to sleep in the same *futon* bedding with the deceased in order to prevent impurities from transferring to others. Death was considered to be an impurity. The fact that friends and acquaintances also attend wakes these days shows that people no longer think of death as something unclean. The sense of departure and comforting the family of the deceased are more relevant issues in modern times.

Thus, those who attend wakes are the ones who were close with the deceased. People often ask me whether they should attend the wake or funeral, but if you were close to the deceased, it is best to attend both rituals. That said, this does not apply, if you're unable to attend the funeral due to a business conflict or something.

通夜は午後六時から七時に始まって一時間から二時間ほど行われることが一般的です。これを「半通夜」と呼びます。通夜ぶるまいは、故人への供養とお清めの意味があるので、すすめられたら参加しましょう。ただし、雑談をしたり、長居することは控えます。

　葬儀は、遺族や近親者で弔（とむら）って故人を成仏させるための儀式です。友人や知人が故人との別れを告げる儀式が告別式です。

　還骨勤行（かんこつごんぎょう）（火葬を終えて骨に還った故人を祭壇に迎える儀式）や初七日法要の後、「精進落とし」（しょうじん）の席が設けられることが一般的です。現代では葬儀関係者の労をねぎらうという意味が強いですが、本来「精進」とは仏教において、生臭（なまぐさ）ものを断ち、身を清めて修行に努めることをいいます。この精進の期間が過ぎて日常に戻ることが精進落としなのです。

　通夜、葬儀（告別式）、いずれも故人の死を悼み、ご冥福を祈り、残されたご遺族をいたわるこころが伴っていることが弔問者には欠かせません。

　帰宅後は、手を洗い、塩を身体の前と後ろにかけてから家に入ります。前述のように死はけがれと考えらえていたことの名残で、水や塩は清めの意味があります。

Today, it is common to host *han-tsuya* "half wake", starting at six or seven o'clock in the evening and lasting for one hour or two. Dinner and drinks served after a wake provide a way to respond to and purify the deceased's soul. If you are asked to stay, please join as much as possible, but be mindful not to talk too much or stay too long.

A funeral is a ritual among families and relatives for the deceased to attain Buddhahood and rest peacefully. The final service is where friends and acquaintances bid farewell to the deceased.

After that, it is commonly followed by a ritual to bring the ashes of the deceased to the alter and another supper and drinks on the seventh day after one's death. The second supper now has the purpose of treating those who helped out with the funeral, but originally it was the meal allowing oneself meat, fish or alcohol after a period of abstaining.

Whether a wake, funeral or final service, the essential aspect of attending these rituals are to mourn the deceased, pray for their peace in the next world and console the family of the deceased.

When returning to your home, it is customary to wash hands and scatter salt over the front and back of your body before entering the house. It is the remnant of the fact that death was considered an impurity and water and salt represent purification.

33

葬式のときの服装について
教えてください。

　通夜の服装は、亡くなることを予期していなかったという表現でもあることから、紺や濃いグレーなどの平服で伺います。そのような場合でも、アクセサリーは外し、濃い色の口紅をつけているときにはできるかぎり薄くするように努めましょう。あらかじめ日時が伝えられている場合は喪服を着用します。

　また喪服は、黒色ならばよいというものではありません。男女ともに少しでも光沢のある素材は避けます。ボタンも光沢がないものを選びます。

　男性は黒のスーツにシャツは白、ネクタイ、靴、靴下は黒の無地、カフスボタンは黒石製のものを着けます。仕事の途中での出席など、ダークスーツでないと難しいことがあるかもしれません。そのようなときには、濃紺や濃いグレーのスーツで、シャツは白、ネクタイや小物は黒が基本ですが、黒に近い地味なものであればよいでしょう。

　女性は、夏場でも襟元が詰まったものでノースリーブは避けて長めの半袖を着用します。深いお辞儀をすることが想定されるため、スカート丈は膝上でなく、膝が隠れる程度のものにします。ストッキングは正礼装でなければ黒でなく肌色でもよいとされていますが、個人的には黒が好ましいように思います。ハンドバッグ、靴はプレーンな黒色のものを選びましょう。本来は布製が望ましいですが、艶や飾りがない革製でもよいです。

What should I wear to a funeral?

For a wake, to express the sense of surprise that you were not expecting the misfortune, you can attend in casual clothes in darker colors such as navy or dark gray. Still, it is best not to wear any accessories or bright lipstick. If the day for a wake is arranged beforehand, you are expected to wear mourning attire.

The dress code for mourning garments is, in addition to the color black, that both men and women should avoid wearing shiny materials such as buttons.

Men can wear a black suit and white shirt with black tie, plain socks, shoes and cuff buttons all in black. In case you are coming directly from work, the best you can do may be a dark suit. Dark navy or dark gray and a white shirt with blackish tie and other accessories are acceptable, if not with black tie and accessories.

Women can wear a conservative dress – not too wide around the neck. In the summer, half sleeves are acceptable but no tank top. As you are probably going to bow deeply, it is best for the skirt to be long enough to cover your knees. Stockings can be your skin color unless you are wearing formal dress, but I personally think it is better to wear black stockings for any funerary occasions. Handbags and shoes are best if plain black and ideally made of cotton, but as long as it is not shiny and decorative, leather is acceptable.

34

焼香、玉串、献花について
教えてください。

仏式の席では、弔問者は焼香をします。焼香の回数については宗派によって異なりますが、基本的には周囲に合わせることが大切です。また小笠原流では、真摯な気持ちを込めることができるならば一回でもよいとしています。

　焼香、玉串（榊の枝に木綿または紙を切ってつくる紙垂をつけたもの）、献花の基本となる作法は次の通りです。

《焼香》
□抹香
①遺族や僧侶に一礼し、焼香台に進む
②焼香台の数歩手前で遺影に向かって合掌礼
③右手で抹香を取るが、このとき左手を添える
④右手でつまんだ抹香を左手で受けるようにして、目の高さで押しいただく
⑤抹香を静かに香炉に入れて手向け、合掌礼をし、下がってから遺族、僧侶に一礼する

□線香（基本は抹香と同様）
①遺族や僧侶に一礼し、線香台の手

34

What do I need to know about manners at funerals?

For a Buddhist funeral, you are expected to offer incense, a branch of a sacred tree and a flower to mourn the deceased. The number of times to burn the incense depends on the Buddhist sect, but it is best to do the same as others do. In the Ogasawara tradition, as long as you are offering sincerely, one time is adequate.

Here are the basic manners for the offerings.

《*Shoko* "offering incense"》
Makko "incense powder"
1 Bow once to the family of the deceased and the monk, walk toward the table for offering incense.
2 Stop a few steps before the table and join your hands in prayer toward the picture of the deceased.
3 Pick up the powdered incense with your right hand. Remember to use your left hand to guide the right hand.
4 Bring your right hand with the support of your left hand to eye level.
5 Place the incense in the incense burner and step back to bow once again to the family of the deceased and the monk.

Senko "incense stick"   *The basic principle is the same as incense powder.
1 Bow once to the family of the deceased and the monk, walk toward the table for offering incense, join your hands in prayer toward the picture of the deceased a few steps before the table, pick

前で合掌礼をしてから、線香を右手で取って火をつける

②線香を左手に持ち替えて右手であおいで火を消す。息を吹きかけて消してはならない

③線香を右手に持ち替えて線香台に立て、合掌礼をし、下がって遺族、僧侶に一礼する

《玉串奉奠の仕方》

①玉串を丁寧に受け取り、胸の高さに捧げて持ち、霊前に進む

②献花台の前で玉串を押しいただき、一礼する

③玉串を時計回りに90度回して自分に対して正面を向ける

④根元が霊前を向くように、180度回す

⑤玉串を台に静かに置く

⑥二礼二拍手一礼してから下がる。このときの拍手は忍び手（音を鳴らさない）とすること

《献花》

①花を丁寧に受け取り、献花台に進む

②献花台の数歩手前で一礼してから、花の正面が霊前に向くように時計回りに取り回す

③花を台に静かに置き、遺影に目を向け、故人への祈りを込めて一礼して下がる

up the incense with your right hand and light it.

2　Re-hold the incense in the left hand and put out the flame by waving your right hand. Never blow.

3　Change it back to your right hand and place it into the incense holder. After joining your hands in prayer, step back and bow once again to the family of the deceased and the monk.

《*Tamagushi Hoten* "offering a branch of a sacred tree"》

1　Receive the branch politely. Hold it in front of your chest and walk toward the alter.

2　At the stand, bring the branch to eye level and bow.

3　Rotate the branch 90 degrees so the front faces you.

4　Rotate it 180 degrees so that the root faces the alter.

5　Gently place the branch on the stand.

6　Bow twice, clap hands twice and bow again before returning to your seat. When clapping hands, try not to make any sound.

《*Kenka* "offering a flower"》

1　Receive the flower politely and walk toward the flower table.

2　Take a bow a few steps before the table and rotate the flower clock wise so the front of the flower faces the alter.

3　Gently place the flower on the table, look at the picture of the de ceased bow and pray before returning to your seat.

35

通夜や告別式には
お金を持参するのですか？

日本では慶事のみならず、弔事の席にも金子包み（不祝儀袋）を持参いたします。慶事では新札が望ましいのに対して、悲しみの席においては使われた紙幣を用いるほうがよいとされます。なぜなら新札は、亡くなることを予期し、前もって準備していたかのような印象を与えると考えられるからです。しかしながら、使いまわされて汚れた紙幣は、受け取る側として気持ちのよいものではありません。そこで、新札を一折してから包むことをおすすめいたします。

金子包みの裏側の上下の重ね方は、まず下から上に向けて折ってから、上から下に被せます。これにより、悲しみで顔を伏せていることを示すともいわれます。

金子包みの表書きは、目に強くなく、かつ悲しみの涙で墨が薄れていると表現することからも、薄墨で記しましょう。最近は、薄墨の筆ペンも市販されています。

表書きについて、仏式は「御香料」、神式は「御玉串料」「御榊料」、キリスト教は「御花料」とするのが一般的です。「御霊前」はおおむね宗派を問わず用いることができます（浄土真宗は御仏前）。

紙幣を直接包む内包みには、遺族側が整理する際にわかりやすいように、金額や名前のほかに住所を書いておくとよいかと思います。

金子包みは、紫、紺、灰色などの帛紗に包んで持参するのが好ましいでしょう。

Should we bring gift money to a wake or funeral?

In Japan, you are expected to offer gift money not only for ceremonial but for funerary occasions, too. Unlike ceremonial occasions, it is considered to be thoughtful to present used bills, because using new bills may bring the impression that you were expecting the misfortune to occur. That said, receiving used bills is not so pleasant. It is best to use new bills but fold and unfold them before wrapping in the envelope.

The folds on the back of the envelope should be made in a certain way. First fold the bottom of the envelope upward and fold the top part to cover the first fold. Some say, the folds represent how you are lying face down in mourning.

When writing on the front of the envelopes, it is best to use a thin black ink. It expresses that your tears of grief have faded the ink. You can purchase a thin black ink pen at stationary stores.

You can write 御香料 (charge for incense) for Buddhist ceremony, 御玉串料 or 御榊料 (charge for sacred branch) for Shinto ceremony, and 御花料 (charge for flowers) for a Christian ceremony. You can use 御霊前 (for the spirit of the deceased) for any Buddhist sect, except the Jodo Shinshu, which uses 御仏前 (before the Buddha).

It is best to note the amount of money, your name and address on the inside envelope so that it is easier for the family of the deceased to organize later.

You are expected to bring the money envelope wrapped in either a purple, navy or gray *fukusa*.

36

「神仏習合」とは何ですか。神社と寺院を参拝する際に違いはありますか？

　本に古来より存在する神の信仰と外来の仏教が融合調和した形態、それを神仏習合と呼びます。神身離脱といって、日本の神々は人間のように悩み苦しんでおり、仏教によって救済されるという思想があり、神社内に神宮寺（神社に付属する仏教寺院）が建てられて神前でお経が読まれました。また寺院内に鎮守社として神社が建てられることもありました。

　その後、江戸時代には神仏分離政策が行われ、明治初年には神仏分離令が公布、それにともない奈良時代から続いた神仏習合は禁止されました。国家神道（国家権力の保護によって神社と皇室の神道が結合し成立した神道）のもとで、明治神宮や靖国神社などが創建され、国民は天皇崇拝と神社信仰を義務づけられましたが、1945年の敗戦後に国家神道は廃止、政教分離（国家と宗教とを分離させる憲法上の原則）が行われました。

　次に、参拝のしかたについてご紹介いたします。まず、神社も寺院も午前中に参拝することをおすすめいたします。なぜなら、大切なことは一日の始めに優先させる、さらに参拝する人が多いと邪気が集まるので早い時間帯のほうが好ましい、とも考えられるからです。

What is syncretism? What do I need to know about visiting shrines and temples?

Syncretism of *kami* "Japanese gods" and Buddhas is the fusion of the older local Shinto beliefs and the newer foreign Buddhist beliefs. There was the idea that the Japanese gods were lost and in need of liberation through Buddhism like any other beings, and temples were built on shrine properties. Also, sutras were read in front of the altar. Sometimes, shrines were built on temple grounds.

In the Edo period, the government began to separate Shinto and Buddhism, and in the Meiji period (1868 – 1912), the government issued the separation order. As a result, the custom of syncretism since the 8th century was banned. Under the name of State Shinto where Imperial Japan used the native folk tradition of Shinto as their ideology, Meiji Shrine and Yasukuni Shrine were founded and Japanese people were obliged to worship Shintoism and the Emperor as a divine being. After Japan lost World War II in 1945, State Shinto was abolished, and the state and religion were separated under law.

Here are the basic manners for visiting shrines and temples. It is better to visit shrines and temples in the morning as you should prioritize important affairs first thing in the morning. It is also better in the sense that the more people visit a temple or shrine, the more evil spirits start to gather. You want to make a visit while the ground is still pure.

【神社の参拝の流れ】

□鳥居をくぐるときに一礼。参道の中央は神様がお通りになるので、左右どちらかに寄ってくぐる。

□手水舎（ちょうずや・ちょうずしゃ）で心身を清める。本来は川や海で心身を清める禊を、この手水舎で簡略化して行うことになる。

《清め方について》

・柄杓を右手で取って水をすくい、左手をすすいで清める

・柄杓を左手に持ち替えて水をすくい、右手をすすいで清める

・柄杓を右手に持ち替えて水をすくい、左手で水を受けて口をすすぐ。このとき、柄杓に口をつけないように注意する

・左手を清め、柄杓を立てて柄を清める

・柄杓をもとにあった場所に伏せてから置く

□参拝は二礼二拍手一礼が基本だが、神社によっては拍手の回数が異なる場合がある。感謝のこころを持つことが大切である。

《参拝について》

・一礼し、賽銭を入れて鈴を鳴らす。賽銭を入れる際の音、鈴の音は参拝者の邪気を祓い、神霊の発動を願うともいわれる。また賽銭は神仏に願ったことが成就したことへの感謝を表す供物ととらえられる

・姿勢を正し、深いお辞儀を二回行う

・両手を胸の高さで合わせて二回、拍手する

・深いお辞儀を一回行う

□戻って鳥居をくぐるときは、本殿に向き直ってから一礼する。

【寺院の参拝の流れ】

【Visiting Shrines】

Bow once before walking through the *torii* "gate". Since the middle of the approach to the shrine is the path for the gods, you should walk on the one side of the approach.

Purify yourself at the water ablution pavilion. Originally purification was done at a stream or seashore. Rinsing your hands at the water pavilion is a simplified style of the original act.

《How to purify yourself》

· Pick up a ladle with your right hand and scoop some water. Purify your left hand with the water.

· Transfer the ladle to your left hand and scoop water again. Purify your right hand with the water.

· Transfer the ladle again to your right hand and scoop more water. Pour the water into your left hand and rinse your mouth with the water. Make sure not to touch the ladle with your lips.

· Rinse your left hand and the hold the handle of the ladle vertically so the leftover water trickles down the shaft.

· Place the ladle back on the basin with the scoop facing down.

The basic way to make a prayer is to bow twice, clap your hands twice and bow again, but the number of times clapping may depend on particular shrines. The most important thing is to pray with a sense of gratitude.

《How to make a prayer》

· Bow once, offer coin money into the offertory chest and ring the bell. The sound the coins and bells make are believed to purify the visitor's malice and to let the spirit know you are there. The money is the offering to represent your gratitude when your wish comes true.

· Assume a proper posture and bow deeply twice.

□山門の前で一礼する。山門に敷居があるときは踏まないように。

　神社のように参道の中央は仏様の通り道、という決まりはないともいわれるが、謙虚な気持ちで中央を歩くことを自然に避けることが好ましい。

□手水舎での清め方の基本は神社と同様。

《参拝について》

・燭台（しょくだい）と香炉（こうろ）がある場合は献灯と献香（けんとう）をする。線香の煙は心身を清めるともいわれる

・一礼してから賽銭を入れる。鰐口（わにぐち）（仏堂の軒先に吊り下げられた音響具）がある場合は鳴らす。寺院での賽銭は前述の通り、神社と同様に感謝を表し、お布施の意味があるともいわれる

・胸の前で合掌し、祈る。合掌は、仏様と一体になることを示すともいわれる

・一礼する。最後まで感謝のこころを忘れずに

□戻って山門をくぐるときは、本堂に向き直ってから一礼する。

　神社、寺院いずれも神仏に対する感謝のみならず、参拝にきている他の人々への配慮なども忘れずに、神聖な場所にふさわしいふるまいをこころがけていただきたいと思います。

・Clap your hands twice in front of your chest.
・Bow once again deeply.
　Before walking back through the *torii* gate, bow once facing toward the shrine.

【Visiting Temples】
　Bow once before walking through the temple gate. Make sure not to step on the threshold. Unlike visiting shrines, there is no written rule about not walking on the middle of the path, but it is best to avoid doing so out of humility.
　The basics for how to purify yourself are the same as when visiting shrines.

《How to make a prayer》
・When there is a candle holder and incense burner, offer a candle and incense. The smoke from the burning incense is believed to purify your body and mind.
・Bow once and offer money into the offertory chest. If there is a gong, ring the gong. Offering money at temples is a sign of your gratitude just like at a shrine, but also is your donation to the temple.
・Join your hands in front of your chest and pray. Joining hands is believed to symbolize that you are united with the Buddha.
・Bow once again. Sustain your sense of gratitude throughout the prayer.

　Before walking back through the gate, bow once facing toward the temple.

　Whether shrines or temples, please do not forget your sense of gratitude toward deities and Buddhas when visiting, and be mindful of other visitors. The idea is to respect sacred places and behave appropriately when visiting them.

年中行事の
「なぜ」

Annual Festivals

四季それぞれのさかりだけを楽しむのではなく、
季節の走りや名残にこそ美しさを
感じることのできる日本人にとって、
古来より年中行事は生活に密着していました。
現代では形骸化してしまった年中行事もありますが、
自然の驚異を感じながら自然に感謝し、
家族や周囲の人が健やかに過ごすことができるようにと
願いながら行う、素敵な風習をご紹介いたします。

正月

　元日（一月一日）には日の出とととともに、農耕民の神である歳神様がいらっしゃるとされてきました。大晦日（十二月三十一日）に一度おまいりすることを除夜詣といいます。一度帰宅し、年が明けてから初詣に行くことが昔は行われていましたが、現在は初詣にのみ行く人が多いのではないかと思います。

　歳神様を迎えるために、門や玄関には門松やしめ飾りを飾ります。松は依代といって、神様が降臨してよりつく（宿る）ところであり、家のなかに飾る松にも、同じ意味が込められています。しめ飾りは、歳神様の訪れる神域を示し、またその場所は清浄であることを示します。

　お正月飾りの飾りつけは、十二月二十九日と三十一日は避けます。なぜなら、二十九日は「九」が「苦」に通じ、三十一日では「一夜飾り」になってしまうからです。したがって、二十八日までに行うことが望ましいのです。

152

Japanese people not only celebrate the best of each season, but also appreciate a sense of the beginning and ending of the four seasons. Traditional annual festivals showcase such sensitivities. Many festivals have lost substance over the years but let me introduce here some enchanting ones that are the embodiment of people's understanding and appreciation of nature and their hopes for the health and prosperity of their families and friends, to name a few.

Shogatsu "New Year"

In Japan, people believe *toshi-gami* "the god of agriculture" visits their homes on New Year's day (Jan. 1). Visiting a shrine to make a prayer on New Year's eve (Dec. 31) is called *joya-mode* and making a visit again after the New Year comes is called *hatsu-mode*. People used to do both after returning home once from *joya-mode* but it is now more common to perform only *hatsu-mode*.

Many people decorate their gates or front doors with pine branches and *shime-nawa* "sacred rope" to welcome *toshi-gami*. Pine is a material by which the spirit is summoned. Some people decorate with pine branches inside their houses for the same reason. *Shime-nawa* represents the area where *toshi-gami* may descend and indicates that the area is purified.

You should avoid decorating for the New Year on December 29th and 31st, because the number nine, pronounced "*ku*", is a homonym for suffering in Japanese and is considered to bring bad luck. Getting ready for the New Year on the 31st at the last minutes shows a lack of respect for the spirits. So it best to have your house decorated for the New Year by December 28th.

Kagami mochi "a round and layered rice cake" is used inside the house as a part of the New Year's celebration. The round shape is be-

さて、室内に飾る鏡餅（かがみもち）は、魂（たましい）をかたどって丸いかたちをしていると いわれます。またお餅が重なっているのは、福が重なるようにとも考え られていますが、お餅そのものが古くから神饌（しんせん）（供物（くもつ））であり、晴れの 日には欠かせないものです。鏡餅は鏡開きといって、一月十一日、ま たは十五日頃に下げ、小豆（あずき）のお汁粉やお雑煮などにして食べます。

　お正月といえば、おせち料理も欠かせません。おせち料理とは「節（せち） 日（び）」に供える「節供（せちく）」のことで、もとは季節の変わり目である節ごとに 食べるものでした。また家事から主婦を休ませるための保存食でもあ ったのです。黒豆は豆に働く、かずのこは子孫繁栄、海老は長寿、昆 布は喜ぶ、田作りは五穀豊穣（ごこくほうじょう）など、それぞれに意味があります。

　おせち料理とともに三が日（一日から三日）に食べるお雑煮は、歳神 様にお供えしたものを神棚から降ろしていただく、というのが起源とも いわれます。地域によって、すまし汁やみそ仕立て、切り餅と丸餅など、 様々な種類のお雑煮が伝えられています。

　お屠蘇（とそ）には、蘇（悪鬼）を屠る（ほふ）（打ち負かす）という意味が込められて います。疲れた胃腸を整える効果もあり、スーパーなどで「屠蘇散（とそさん）」 を購入することができます。屠蘇散をお酒やみりんに浸してつくります。 三が日の間はぜひ召し上がっていただきたいものです。

　お正月飾りは松の内（歳神様がいらっしゃる期間）の間のみのものです ので、主に関東では七日前後、関西では十五日前後に外します。 二十日正月といって、お正月行事のすべてはこの日までとされます。

lieved to be shaped round to represent the human soul and they are layered to "pile up" good fortune. Rice cakes have been an offering to the Japanese gods since ancient times and people always eat or decorate rice cakes on special occasions in Japan. *Kagami mochi* is brought down on the day of *kagami biraki*, January 11th or around the 15th, and eaten in *oshiruko* "sweet red-bean soup" or *ozoni* "New Year's vegetable soup."

Another indispensable item for New Year's celebrations in Japan is *osechi* "New Year's dishes." *Osechi* literally means offering for seasonal festivals and people used to eat *osechi* at the change of every season. Osechi are also preserved dishes which allow the housewives to take a break from daily cooking. Each *osechi* ingredient has a particular meaning. For example, black beans represent working hard since beans and work hard in Japanese are homonyms. Herring roe symbolizes fertility, shrimp longevity, kelp joy and dried sardines a great harvest.

Ozoni is another dish served during the first three days of the New Year as part of the celebration. It is said the origin was to share the rice cake offered to *toshi-gami* among family members after taking it down from the household alter. Recipes for *ozoni* vary from region to region. Some places serve it with a clear soup and others with *miso* soup. The shape of the rice cake can be square or round depending on the area.

Otoso "spiced *sake*" traditionally drunk during New Year's celebrations literally means to defeat demons. It helps to condition the digestive system which may be irritated from New Year's celebrations. *Toso-san* "a combination of several medical herbs" can be purchased at the supermarket and you can soak the mix in *mirin* to make *otoso*. It is recommended to take *otoso* during the first three days of the New Year.

New Year's decorations in the house should only be on display while the toshi-gami is visiting. In the Kanto area they are taken down around January 7th and in Kansai around January 15th. All New

五節供

　ひなまつりやこどもの日、七夕はご存じの方が多いですが、日本には一月、三月、五月、七月、九月と年五回の節供があります。節には悪鬼が跳梁して災いをなす、と考えられていました。したがって、節供の日は、単に祝うだけでなく、厄を祓い、五穀豊穣と健康を願う大切な日として過ごしてはいかがでしょうか。

一月七日 ｜ 人日の節供（七草の節供）

　七日を人日といい、七日正月、若菜節ともいわれます。

　「せり、なずな、ごぎょう、はこべら、ほとけのざ、すずな、すずしろ」が一般的な七草で、この日に七草のお粥を食べることには災厄を除こうとする願いが込められています。消化の良いお粥は、お正月の間に食べ過ぎ飲み過ぎの胃腸をいたわる、先人の知恵ともいえましょう。

　なぜ七日を人日と呼ぶようになったかについては、

「一日鶏、二日狗、三日猪、四日羊、五日牛、六日馬、七日人、八日穀これなり」

と小笠原流の伝書に記されています。

三月三日 ｜ 上巳の節供（桃の節供）

　本来は旧暦三月最初の巳の日を指していたものが、いつしか三月三日に固定されました。

　雛は形代（神霊の代わり）として作った人形で、自分の身体を撫でた人形を水に流すことで災厄をまぬがれると考えられていたのです。そのような意味合いが薄らぎ、立ち雛から座り雛へと変化し、飾りとしての雛人形が用いられるようになったのは、江戸時代からといわれてい

Year's festivities end by the 20th.

Go-sekku "the five seasonal festivals"

Including well-known festivals such as *hina matsuri* "girl's festival", *kodomo no hi* "boy's festival" and *tanabata* "weaver's festival", people traditionally celebrate five seasonal festivals in January, March, May, July and September in Japan. It was believed evil spirits would come out on auspicious dates to cause trouble. Therefore it is important to not only celebrate these festive days but to also drive away evil spirits and wish for a bountiful harvest and good health.

January 7th: *Jin-jitsu no sekku* **"human day festival"** or *Nana-kusa no sekku* **"festival of seven spring herbs"**

Also known as *wakana no sechi* "young green festival."

Oenanthe javanica, shepherd's purse, cudweed, chickweed, nipplewort, turnip and radish are the most common seven herbs and eating a rice gruel that contains the seven herbs on the 7th day of the first month of the year is believed to ward off evil. Since ancient times it is said that eating it helps digest all your New Year's over indulgences.

Why is the 7th day refereed to as *jin-jitsu*? In the Book of Ogasawara it is written that the "the first day is for chickens, the second day is for dogs, the third day is for boar, the fourth day is for sheep, the fifth day is for cows, the sixth day is for horses, the seventh day is for humans, and the eighth day is for grain."

March 3rd: *Joshi no sekku* **"early day of the snake festival"** or *Momo no sekku* **"peach festival"**

Originally it was held on the first day of the snake in March of the old lunar calendar, but at some point, it became fixed on March 3rd.

People celebrate this day by displaying *hina* dolls. *Hina* dolls were originally made to summon the spirits. The *hina* were dolls that were originally made to represent divine spirits. It is said that by rubbing

ます。

　桃は邪気を祓う仙木で、花や葉を浸した桃酒を飲むことは、延命を祈るだけでなく、血圧を整えて強心健胃にも通じるとされています。

　また、この時期には古くから草餅が食べられますが、もとはよもぎでなく、母子草（春の七草のひとつであるごぎょう）を用いていたという説があります。

五月五日｜端午の節供（菖蒲の節供）

　上巳と同様に、旧暦五月最初の午の日を指していましたが、現在は五月五日に定まっています。菖蒲にかけて尚武（武勇を大切にすること）の節供ともいわれます。

　男子の出世を祈ることから立身出世のシンボルとして鯉のぼりが飾られます。兜飾り、武者人形などと相まって、江戸時代に男子の節供として定着しました。

　五色の糸を用いた薬玉や粽も端午の節供に欠かせないものであり、菖蒲の葉を浮かべた菖蒲湯に入ることも、この時期ならではの風習です。

　柏餅を食べるのは、柏の葉は新芽が出るまで古い葉が落ちないため、子孫繁栄に繋がるとされているからです。

七月七日｜七夕の節供

　七夕は、疫病を避けるため旧暦七月七日に索餅（小麦とお米を練って紐状にしたものを綯ったお菓子）を主上に献じた、という中国の故事からきています。現在この日に素麺を食べたり贈ったりするのは、この索餅がもととなっているからです。

　機屋に籠って神の来臨を待つ乙女が織姫で、翌朝神様がお帰り

them against your body and setting them afloat was a way to escape from disaster and misfortune. The original meaning has somewhat faded and the standing position of the dolls became seated, then people started to decorate the dolls during the Edo period.

A peach tree is believed to be a spiritual tree which removes evil. Drinking peach wine, made of peach flowers and leaves, is thought to be good for longevity, controlling blood pressure and strengthening the stomach.

Kusa-mochi "rice cake mixed with mugwort" is a popular sweet around this season. Some say it used to be cudweed, one of the seven herbs, instead of mugwort.

May 5th: *Tango no sekku* **"the first day of the horse festival" or** *Shobu no sekku* **"Iris festival"**

Similar to *joshi no sekku*, it used to be held on the first day of the horse in May on the old lunar calendar, but it is now fixed on May 5th. The festival celebrates valor and the iris a homonym with "martial spirit" in Japanese. During the Edo period it became a festival devoted to praying for the prosperity of boys. A symbol of courage and strength, *Koinobori* (carp shaped banners) along with *samurai* helmets and dolls are also displayed.

Kusu-dama "an ornamental ball created by using five colored strings" and *chimaki* "a sweet wrapped in bamboo leaves" are associated with the festival. It is also customary in this season to take a *shobu-yu*, a bath steeped with the leaves of irises.

Kashiwa-mochi "rice cake wrapped in oak leaf" is a seasonal sweet in May. Since oak trees don't lose their old leaves until the new leaves come out and it is believed to bring prosperity to one's descendants.

July 7th: *Tanabata no sekku* **"weaver's festival"**

This festival originates from a Chinese tradition where people used to offer *sakubei* "twisted flour cake" to their masters to ward off the

になるときに、村人は禊を行ってその汚れを持ち帰っていただく、という信仰が織姫彦星の伝説と結びついて現在の七夕をつくり上げました。

笹竹に願い事を記した短冊を飾りますが、この笹竹を川や海に流す風習があるのも、七夕が祓いの日であることを物語っています。

九月九日｜重陽の節供（菊の節供）

一般に馴染みの薄い節供ですが、菊の節供とも呼ばれ、菊見や菊人形など菊を愛でる日でもあります。

陰陽道では奇数を陽、偶数を陰としますが、陽の数のうちで最も大きな九が重なることから重陽と呼ばれるようになりました。平安時代から宮中では詩を詠じ、飲むと災厄から逃れられるとされる菊花酒が嗜まれていました。

現代にも伝わる御九日（おくにち、おくんち）という収穫祭は、農民の間から始まりました。この時期に栗を食べることも中国から伝わり、日本でも栗ご飯を食べる風習があります。

節分

立春の前日（二月三日頃）が節分ですが、本来は立春、立夏、立秋、立冬それぞれの前日を全て節分といいます。宮中行事の追儺の行事が節分の起源といわれます。厄を祓うことから「鬼は外」と、福を取り込むことから「福は内」といって豆を投げます。豆は魔滅に繋がるともいわれます。豆まきの行事は江戸時代から一般的に行われるようなりました。豆まきの後は、一年の無病息災を祈り、年齢の数だけ豆を食べます。

plague on the seventh day of the seventh month of the old lunar calendar. Today, people eat or exchange somen noodles as a gift based on the tradition.

The Chinese story of a maiden waiting for the god's descendant in the weaving shop and the villagers purifying themselves and asking the god to take their sins away when returning was combined with the Japanese legend of *Orihime* and *Hikoboshi* and formed today's festival.

People hang their wishes written on strip of paper on a bamboo tree for the festival. Some places throw the tree into the ocean or river. It is a remnant of the original notion that the festival was a day for purification.

September 9th: *Joyo no sekku* **"dual ultimate active number festival" or** *Kiku no sekku* **"chrysanthemum festival"**

Many people may be unfamiliar with this festival, but it is a day to appreciate viewing chrysanthemum flowers or dolls made from chrysanthemum flowers.

According to the Chinese notion of yin and yang, odd numbers are regarded as active numbers and even numbers are passive. Among the numbers, nine is the ultimate, so that a dual nine means the highest level of activeness. Since the Heian period, people at court composed poetry and drank liquor made from the chrysanthemum, which was believed to dispel evil.

The harvest festival called *oku-nichi* "the ninth day of a month" started among farmers and is practiced even to this day. The tradition of eating chestnuts around this time of year was introduced from China and people eat chestnut rice in modern Japan.

Setsubun

Most people refer to *setsubun* as the day before the beginning of spring, but originally the days before summer, fall and winter were also called *setsubun*. A ceremony of driving evil spirits out at court

彼岸（春、秋）

　春分の日（三月二十一日頃）、秋分の日（九月二十三日頃）を中心に、それぞれ前後三日間の合わせて七日間がお彼岸です。仏教における本来の彼岸の意味は、煩悩に打ち勝って悟りの境地に達することです。西方浄土といって、極楽浄土は真西にあり、春分と秋分の日は太陽が真西に沈み、現世と極楽浄土が最も近づくことから、この日に先祖の成仏を願って供養し、お墓参りをするようになりました。

　初日を彼岸入り、最終日を彼岸明けといいます。春のお彼岸にはぼた餅、秋のお彼岸にはおはぎをお墓や仏壇にお供えし、その後下ろしていただきます。

盆

　正式には盂蘭盆会といい、七月または八月に行われます。先祖の霊（魂）をお迎えして祀る行事です。サンスクリット語で「逆さに吊るされた苦しみ」という意味のある盂蘭盆は、お釈迦様の弟子・目連の母が餓鬼道に落ちて苦しんでいたため、お釈迦様の教えにしたがって供養したことに由来します。

　現在は一般的に七月（八月）十三日の精霊迎えから十六日の精霊送りまでの期間、盆棚を設けて先祖供養を行います。十三日までにお墓参りをして、盆棚を設けて先祖の霊が迷わないようにと迎え火を焚きます。盆棚は、仏前に小机を置き、すのこなどを敷いて位牌を移し、生花、果物や野菜、そうめん、団子などをお供えします。先祖が現世とあの世を往来する乗り物をきゅうりやなすで作って飾ります。祖霊を迎えた後は、朝昼晩の三回、食事やお水を供えます。十五日

is believed to be the origin of it. In order to drive evil spirits away, people throw roasted soybeans while saying *Oni wa soto, Fuku wa uchi* "demons out, fortune in." Beans are *mame* in Japanese and puns with *mametsu* which means ending evil. The custom of throwing beans has become popular among the common people since the Edo period. After throwing beans, people eat the same number of beans as their age hoping for good luck in the year to come.

Higan (Spring & Fall)

Two periods of seven days with the middle day falling on the spring or autumn equinox, around March 21st and September 23rd.

The origin of *higan* is the attempt to gain enlightenment by being free from earthly desires in the Japanese Buddhist tradition. Japanese Buddhism believes the pure land lies in the west. Since the sun sets due west on the days of the spring and autumn equinox, people thought it was the time this mortal world and the pure land became closest. In the hope that their ancestors may attain Buddhahood, Japanese people pay a visit to their family graves on these days.

The first day of *higan* week is called *higan-iri* "entering *higan*" and the last day *higan-ake* "ending *higan*." It is customary to offer *bota-mochi* "red bean rice cakes" for the graves and family Buddhist alters in spring and *ohagi* "red bean rice cakes" in fall, and to eat these cakes afterward.

Bon

Bon, taking place in July or August, is a shortened form of *urabon'e*, meaning "hanging upside down" in Sanskrit, and it is a Japanese Buddhist custom to honor the spirits of your ancestors. It originates in the story of Mokuren, one of Buddha's disciples, who helped his mother who was suffering in a realm of hell. Upon Buddha's advice, he made efforts on his mother's behalf and was able to save her to be reborn in a better place.

Today, it is common to celebrate the return of your ancestors' spir-

または十六日の夜、送り火を焚いて祖霊を送ります。

　生見玉（生御霊、生身魂）といって、この時期には健在の親への食物を贈る風習もあります。このときに用いられる魚を盆魚といい、鯖が多いようです。

中元

　古代中国では旧暦で一月十五日を上元、七月十五日を中元、十月五日を下元とし、中元の日は慈悲神様を祀ったといわれています。この中元が前述の盂蘭盆会と結びつき、贈答の習慣が浸透しました。

　一方、日本には鎌倉時代から、八朔の贈答といって八月一日に収穫を祝う風習があり、これを「田の実の節供」とも呼んで農作物を贈り合いました。この風習が武家に伝わると、太刀や馬などの武具が贈答品として用いられるようになったのです。主従や縁故を確認し合う大切な風習であったともいえましょう。

　中元の贈答は、七月初旬から十五日頃までをめどにしますが、八月に行う地域もあります。

月見

　旧暦八月十五日の十五夜、九月十三日の十三夜、この両日の月を愛でることがお月見です。十五夜は里芋をお供えすることから芋名月、また中秋の名月とも呼ばれます。十三夜は豆や栗を供えることから「豆名月」「栗名月」とも呼ばれます。

　どちらか一方の月のみを鑑賞することは「片月見」「片見月」といって、縁起がよくないとされています。

its between July or August 13th to 16th by setting up a *bon-dana* "table for offering." People visit and clean their ancestors' grave by the 13th, set up a *bon-dana* and make a welcome fire to lead the spirits' way. To make a *bon-dana*, you can place a small table on your family alter, move the mortuary tablet to a board, then offer flowers, fruits, vegetable, *somen* noodles, dumplings and more. The vessel for the ancestors' spirits to ride between this world and the afterlife is decorated with cucumbers and eggplants. Once the spirits revisit the alter, you make offerings three times a day – breakfast, lunch and dinner with food and water. On the night of the 15th or 16th, you make another ceremonial fire to see the spirits off.

Some places have a custom called *iki-mitama* to offer food to your living parents during *bon* season. A common fish used for the offering is mackerel.

Chugen

In ancient China, people called January 15th *jo-gen*, July 15th *chugen* and October 15th *ka-gen* according to the old lunar calendar, and they celebrated the god of mercy on the day of *chu-gen*. This tradition met with Japanese *urabon'e* and the custom of exchanging gifts around this time of year has become popular in Japan.

Ever since the Kamakura period, farmers celebrated their harvest on August 1st (Hassaku) by exchanging products from the field. Once this habit was introduced to *samurai* families, they started to exchange weapons such as swords and horses as gifts. It was an important custom for them to confirm their relationship and the bond between the lord and vassal.

Today, it is best to send your gifts starting the first week and be finished around July 15th. In Some regions, people practice *chugen* in August.

七五三

　十一月十五日に、氏神様へ収穫の感謝、こどもの成長と加護を願う行事が七五三です。髪型を改める三歳の髪置の儀、初めて袴をつける五歳の袴着の儀、つけひもを取って初めて本式の帯をつける七歳の帯解の儀があります。

　現在では三歳は男女、五歳は男子、七歳は女子というのが一般的ですが、地方によって異なる場合があります。

　昔は「七歳までは神の子」といわれ、七歳になって初めて霊魂が安定すると考えられていましたが、現代でもこどもが健やかに成長することを願う親の気持ちに変わりはないでしょう。

　また満年齢でお祝いをすることが多いようですが、数え年で行ってもよいのです。

歳暮

　中元とともに、今日も行われている贈答の風習です。一年間の感謝の意を伝えるものですが、お正月の準備が始まる十二月十三日を中心に、二十日頃までに先方へ届くことが基本です。ただし、お正月用の賞味期限が短いものは、もう少し遅くお届けしてもよいでしょう。

　基本的に、中元を差し上げた方には歳暮の品も贈ります。

　中元、歳暮ともにお返しの品は必要ないといわれますが、お礼状は速やかにお送りします。

Tsuki-mi

According to the old lunar calendar *tsuki-mi* (moon viewing) was done on August 15th and the thirteenth night of September. The August moon was called *jugo-ya* (15th night) and the September moon *jusan-ya* (13th night). As people would offer taro on *jugo-ya* it came to be known as *imo meigetsu* (potato moon). It's also known as *chushu no meigetsu* (mid-autumn moon). *Jusan-ya* is celebrated with beans and chestnuts so it is referred to as the *mame meigetsu* (bean moon) or *kuri meigetsu* (chestnut moon).

Viewing only one of the moons is called *kata tsuki-mi* or *katami tsuki* and considered to be bad luck.

Shichi-go-san

Shichi-go-san, meaning seven-five-three, is an event to thank *uji-ga-mi* for the harvest and to wish for children's healthy growth.

People used to change their hair style at the age of three, wear *haka-ma* "men's formal pleated skirt-like pants" at the age of five for the first time and start wearing a formal *obi* belt instead of a child's sash at the age of seven.

Today, it is common to celebrate both girls and boys at the age of three, boys at five and girls at seven, but it can vary from region to region.

In the old days, it was believed all children were a child of god until seven years old and their souls finally became stable at the age of seven. This is no longer the case in modern times, but the fact that parents wish for their children's healthy growth has not changed.

It has also become more common to celebrate the children's actual age instead of their age in the calendar year. However, it is still respectable to celebrate their calendar year ages.

すす払い

　お正月に歳神様をお迎えするには、その前にすすを払って家内を清浄にすることが欠かせません。本来、お正月の準備を始める事始めの日が十二月十三日のすす払いの日なのですが、現代においては年末近くに行われることが多いのではないかと思います。

　この日はお正月飾りに用いる松を山へ伐りに行く松迎えを行ったり、しめ縄を綯うなどの準備をする日でもあるのです。正月迎え、まつならしなどとも呼ばれます。

　すす払いが終わった日の夜にお餅やお団子などを食べる、すす払い祝いという風習もあります。

Seibo

Similar to *chugen*, people also exchange gifts at the end of the year in Japan. Your gift represents your gratitude toward that person for the year and it is best to send the gift between December 13th and the 20th, before the preparations for the New Year begin. If your gift is to be used for the New Year celebration and has a short expiration date, you may send it earlier than usual.

Normally, you send a *seibo* gift for those to whom you sent a *chugen* gift.

A gift in return is not necessary, but it is best to send a thank you note as soon as you receive any gift.

Susu harai

Susu harai means sweeping away the soot. In order to welcome *toshi-gami* in the New Year, it is very important to clean and purify the entire house beforehand. Originally the day of *susu harai* was December 13th, the first day of the New Year's preparations, but it is more common today to clean the house closer to the end of the year.

It is also the day to pick the pine branches for the New Year's decorations and make *shime-nawa*. These decorations are also called *shogatsu mukae* "welcoming the New Year" or *matsu narashi* "pine custom."

There is also a tradition called *susu-harai iwai* "celebrating *susu harai*" in which people eat rice cakes or dumplings in the evening of the day you finish *susu harai*.

着物、浴衣について

着物の由来と、着付けの基本を教えてください。

　明治時代、西洋から伝わった衣服（洋服）を着る人が増えるにつれて、古来からの日本の服を和服と呼ぶようになりました。

　和服と着物は同じような意味で用いられますが、着物は「着るもの」からきており、長着（丈の長い着物）を指すことが多いのです。

　武士が用いていた小袖と呼ばれる着物が、江戸時代になると一般の人々にも普及し、染色の技法も現代に通じるものが確立されました。

　季節に応じて十月から五月は裏地のある袷、六月と九月は裏地のない単、七月から八月は裏地がなく涼しい素材の薄物というのが基本ですが、昨今のように初夏でも暑さが厳しいときなどは、このかぎりではありません。

　さて、着付けは胸元の印象が全体の品格を左右いたします。胸元を広く開ける、あるいは必要以上に衣紋を抜く（襟の後ろを引き下げる）ことはせず、襟元が詰まりすぎても不自然ですのでこれも避けましょう。せっかく美しい着付けであっても、歩くときに裾の乱れに注意しないと肌が見えるなどして品格を損ないます。特に階段の上り下りでは、ふくらはぎが露出しないように気を付けます。上前（着物の前を合わせたときに外側になる部分）を押さえると裾の乱れを防ぐことができます。階段では、腿の力で上り下りするイメージを持つとよいでしょう。袖口を気にせずに手を上にあげたり、前方に出すことも、腕が見えてしまって好ましくありません。そのようなときは、片方の手で袖口をつまむようにします。

Kimono & Yukata

What is the origin of the *kimono?*
What is the proper way to wear a *kimono?*

In Japan, people started to wear western style clothing in the Meiji period (1868 – 1912). It was around that time that the traditional style of clothing began to be called *wafuku* "Japanese style clothing."

Wafuku is nearly synonymous with *kimono* but *kimono*, literally meaning "wearing things", usually refers to ankle-length long garments.

The prototype of today's *kimono* is *kosode*, a type of *kimono* the *samurai* used to wear. The style became popular among common people in the Edo period and the dying technique was developed around the same time.

The basic rules for *kimono* are to wear a lined *kimono* from October to May, an unlined *kimono* from June to September, and a lighter *kimono* with no lining and a cool fabric in July and August. Depending on the weather one doesn't have to adhere to the rules so strictly these days, sometimes it's extremely hot even in the early summer.

When dressing in *kimono*, the way you adjust the neckline determines the grace of your look. You should avoid a plunging line in front or pulling the back of the collar more than necessary. Being too tight around the neck also looks ungraceful. Even when you are wearing it properly, if you are not careful walking, you may degrade yourself by exposing your leg. Be mindful, especially when going up and down the stairs, not to expose your calf. Holding the front of your *kimono* with your hand can prevent the hem from rumpling. When using stairs, think of moving your leg with your thighs instead of with the feet. Waving the sleeves or raising your arms without much caution will expose your arms and is not well-mannered. If you need to move your arms, you can use the other hand to hold the edge of the sleeve.

浴衣はどのような場で着てもよいのですか？
着付けのポイントも教えてください。

　浴衣は平安時代、貴族が蒸し風呂に入るときにやけどをしないため、また汗を取って身体を隠すために用いられたものです。綿の普及によって江戸時代から広まりました。素材が綿ということからも、浴衣はカジュアルな装いであることを忘れないでください。改まった場には絹製の着物が適しています。

　とはいうものの、今まで着物に袖を通す機会がなかった方は、浴衣から試してみるとよいのではないかと思います。胸元の整え方、歩くときの裾への配慮、腕を見せないように袖口をつまむなどのポイントは、前述の通りです。

　浴衣の胸元が崩れたときは、おはしょり（着丈よりも長い部分を腰の辺りで紐で止めて折り返したところ）を下から引くと簡単で効果的です。背中がもたついた場合も、後ろのおはしょりを下に引きます。裾が落ちてきてしまったら、おはしょりを上に持ち上げ、上前を引いて長さを調整いたしましょう。

　次頁より、女性の浴衣の着付けをイラストでご紹介いたしますので、ぜひ、ご自身でお召しになってみてはいかがでしょう。

When do you wear *yukata*?
What is the proper way to wear *yukata*?

Yukata were originally worn by the aristocracy in steam baths to cover and protect their bodies from burning as well as absorbing sweat. In the Edo period, it became popular among common people due to the wider supply of cotton. Don't forget that the *yukata* is a casual garment as it is made of cotton so it is more suitable to wear silk *kimono* to formal occasions.

However, *yukata* are a great way to try *wafuku* for the first time. The important aspects regarding how to wear and move in *yukata* are the same as *kimono*.

When you need to adjust your neckline, it is easy to do so by pulling the tuck around your waist. If you need to fix the backline, you can do the same. If your hem starts to come down, you can pull up the tuck and draw on the front of the *yukata* to adjust the length.

This book includes an illustrated guide for wearing female *yukata*. I hope you will try it!

浴衣の着付け

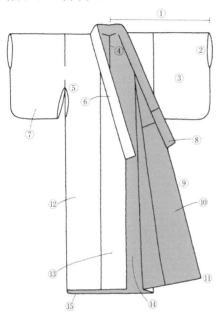

部分名称

① 裄
② 袖口
③ 袖
④ 背縫い
⑤ 身八つ口
⑥ 衿
⑦ 袂
⑧ 衿先
⑨ 褄
⑩ 前身頃（上前）
⑪ 褄先
⑫ 前身頃（下前）
⑬ 衽
⑭ 後ろ身頃
⑮ 裾

準備するもの

浴衣、下着、半幅帯、帯板、伊達締め、腰ひも2〜3本、ウエスト補正用タオル数枚

How to put on a *yukata*

Yukata Parts

1. *Yuki*: Length between the center of the back and the end of the sleeves
2. *Sode-guchi*: Openings of the sleeves
3. *Sode*: Sleeves
4. *Senui*: Back seam
5. *Miyatsu-kuchi*: Openings near the armpits
6. *Eri*: Collar
7. *Tamoto*: Bottom ends of the sleeves
8. *Eri-saki*: Tip of the collar
9. *Tsuma*: Both sides of the *yukata*
10. *Mae-migoro / Uwa-mae*: Front main panel *The exterior panel is called *uwa-mae*
11. *Tsuma-saki*: The tips of the *tsuma*
12. *Mae-migoro / Shita-mae*: Front main panel *The interior panel is called *shita-mae*
13. *Okumi*: Half width strips connecting *mae-migoro* and the collar
14. *Ushiro-migoro*: Back main panels
15. *Suso*: Hem

What you need:

yukata, undergarment, half-width *obi* "belt", *obi-ita* "plate", date-jime "under sash", 2 to 3 *koshi-himo* "cords", a few towels to shape around the waist.

174

下着を着て、補正をする

1. まず、下着を付けます。ウエストのくびれをなくすために、胴にタオルを巻き、腰ひもで固定します。

Preparation

1. Put on the undergarment. Wrap the towels around the waist to flatten the curves of the body and secure the towels with a *koshi-himo*.

2. 腰ひもをきつく締めると苦しくなるので、ゆるまない程度に結びます。

2. Tying the cord too tight can be uncomfortable. Tie it tight enough so that it won't come off easily, but not too tight.

浴衣を着る

3. 浴衣をはおり、左右の衿先をそろえて、衿の中ほどを持ち、身体の中心にあわせて軽く前へ引きます。

Yukata

3. Put on *yukata*. Use one hand to hold both tips of the collar together and the other hand to hold the middle of the collar in front of your body. Pull slightly away from you.

4. もう片方の手で背縫い部分を持ち、背縫いが身体の中心にくるようにします。

4. Let go of the tips of the collar and, using your free hand, feel for the center seam on the back. Adjust the *yukata* so the seam is centered with your back and the sides are even.

5. 両手で衿先を持ち、裾線がくるぶしあたりにくるように調節します。浴衣は涼しげに見えるよう、普通の着物より着丈を短めに着付けるのが基本です。

5. Hold both tips of the collar with both hands and adjust the hem to ankle length. *Yutaka* is worn somewhat shorter than *kimono* to appear cooler in the heat.

6. 次に、左手に持った前身頃（上前）をあわせて、褄の位置を決めます。

6. Bring the left side to your hip and determine where you want the front panel to be.

7. 一度左手を戻して、上前がゆるまないように右手で持った前身頃（下前）をあわせ、左の腰のほうへ巻きこみます。

7. Bring the left side back without loosening it and pull the right side of the garment to your hip bone, and hold it in place with your right hand.

8. 再度、上前を重ねあわせます。このとき、上前の褄先が下前の裾線より2〜3cm短くなるようにします。

8. Cross the left side again to your right hip. Adjust the front side tip to be about an inch shorter than the tip of the inner hem.

9. 押さえている上前の右腰に腰ひもをあて、ひもの中心が前中心にくるようにして、水平に巻きます。

9. Place a *koshi-himo* onto the right hip where you are holding and wrap it around yours hips, then tie a single knot on your side.

10. 腰ひもを脇で結び、余分は挟みこみます。

10. Tuck excess *koshi-himo* under itself.

11. おはしょりの形を整えます。身八つ口から手を入れて、まず身体の前におはしょりをきれいにおろします。

11. Insert your hands into the openings near the armpits and push the extra fabric down over the *koshi-himo*. Adjust the front tuck.

12. 背中心がずれないように注意しながら、後ろのおはしょりも同様にします。

12. Do the same in the back, while keeping the back seam centered.

13. 衿の形を整えてから、胸の下あたりにひも
を巻きます。まず背中心を持って、後ろ衿を、
首との間にこぶしが一つ入るくらい抜き（引き）、
前は、衿のあわせが喉のくぼみにくるように調
節します。

13. Straighten out the collar and wrap another
koshi-himo cord around your upper waist. Pull the
back of the collar away from your neck by pulling
the middle of the back fabric down. There should
be enough space to fit your fist between the collar
and the back of your neck. The collars in the front
should meet below the hollow of your neck.

14. ひもは脇で結んで、余分を挟みこみます。

14. Tie the *koshi-himo* and tuck the excess in.

15. 背中側のひもに両手の人さし指を下から
入れて、前へ移動させながら後ろ身頃のシワ
を脇に向かって伸ばします。

15. Insert your index fingers up under the *koshi-himo* in the back and smooth the wrinkles out by
moving them toward the sides.

16. 前身頃のシワも同様に、脇に向かって伸ば
し、身八つ口でそれぞれの余分を、前身頃分
を上にして重ね合わせます。

16. Do the same in the front and lay the excesses
from the front over the excess from the back at the
openings under the sleeves.

17. 上前と下前のおはしょりの重なりをすっきりさせるため、下前のおはしょりを内側に折り上げ、先をひもに挟むようにして、おはしょりの下部を一重にします。

17. In order to make the front tuck look elegant, fold the underneath tuck up and put the tip under the *koshi-himo*. It helps the bottom part of the tuck to be a single layer and look more lightweight.

伊達締めを巻く

18. 伊達締めの中心を、ウエストよりやや上の身体の正面にあてます。

Date-jime **under sash**

18. Place the center of the *date-jime* onto the middle of your upper waist.

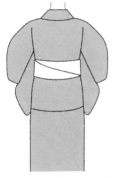

19. 伊達締めの両端を後ろにまわし、斜めに折り返して交差させ、背中を平坦にします。

19. Wrap the *date-jime* around your waist. Fold the sash diagonally to make it flat on your back.

20. 正面で結びます。このとき、ゆるまないように二度からめ、左端を右へ、右端を左へねじるように交差させ、左右の端は伊達締めに挟みこみます。

20. Tie a double knot in front. Twist, cross and tuck both ends under the *date-jime* .

179

たれ
Long End

て
Short End

帯を結ぶ

21. 伊達締めの上に帯板を付けます。

Obi belt
21. Secure the *obi-ita* on top of the *date-jime*.

22. 帯の端から50〜60cmほどを半分に折って、「て」をつくります。この部分を左手に、反対側(「たれ」)を右手に持って、後ろから前へと巻きます。

22. Fold about 20 to 23 inches of one end of the *obi* in half lengthwise. Hold the short end with your left hand and the long end with your right hand.

23.「て」は右肩にあずけ、「たれ」を巻いていきます。

23. Drape the short end over your right shoulder and wrap the long end around your waist.

24. 2周巻いて、「たれ」が前にきたところで、内側斜めに折り上げます。

24. Wrap it around twice and as the long end reaches to the front, fold it up diagonally.

25.「て」を「たれ」の上へおろして、交差させます。

25. Bring the short end down and across the long end.

26.「て」を「たれ」に通して結びます。

26. Loop the short end around the long end and tie a single knot.

27.「て」と「たれ」の結び目をタテにして、今度は「て」を左肩に仮置きします。

27. Hold the knot vertically and drape the short end over your left shoulder.

28. 残った「たれ」で羽根をつくります。

28. The long end will be used to make a bow.

29.「たれ」を胸幅より少し長めにとり、三面の巻きだたみ（すのこだたみ）にします。「たれ」の残りの長さは人によって違うため、長短を加減しましょう。

29. Fold the long end two times so that there are three layers, each a little wider than the breadth of your chest. The length of the long end varies from person to person. Adjust the width to fit you.

30. 羽根の中央に人さし指を置き、上を親指、下を残りの指で押さえて二つの山をつくり、胴に巻いた帯の上のほうにもってきます。

30. Placing the index finger in the center, pinch the top and bottom of the *obi* together with your thumb and the rest of your fingers, so the sides stick out in a bow shape. Bring the bow to the upper part of the *obi*.

31.「て」を羽根の中央部にかぶせるように2回巻きます。

31. Loop the short end tightly around the middle of the bow two times.

32.「て」の先を帯と帯板の間に差し込みながら、半分に折られていた「て」を広げ、帯の下へ引っぱります。

32. Tuck the remaining length of the short end in between the *obi* and *obi-ita*. Unfold the short end and pull it downward towards the bottom of the *obi* belt.

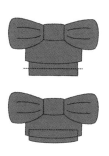

33. 下に出た「て」が長い場合は、帯下から2〜3cm出るくらいまで、内側へ折りこみます。

33. If the tip of the short end sticks out from under of the *obi*, you can fold it inside and leave about an inch length at the bottom.

34. 結びが上を向くように起こすと、帯下から出ていた分が引かれて、帯の中へ隠れます。

34. Pulling the bow knot upward will hide the excess at the bottom of the *obi*.

35. 羽根の先を下げて、左右対称になるように形を整えます。

35. Pull down the wings and adjust the shape symmetrically.

36. 帯を数回に分けて、右回りで後ろへまわします。逆にまわすと、衿元や上前が開いて着崩れてしまうので注意しましょう。

36. Rotate the knot to the side and to your back clockwise. Turning it around the other way would loosen the neckline and the top panel.

小笠原敬承斎 おがさわら・けいしょうさい

先代宗家 小笠原惣領家第三十二世 小笠原忠統の実姉(村雲御所瑞龍寺十二世門跡 小笠原日英尼公)の真孫。聖心女子専門学校卒業後、英国留学。平成8年、小笠原流礼法宗家に就任。聖徳大学・聖徳大学短期大学部客員教授。各地での指導・講演を行う。著書多数。

Keishosai Ogasawara

Granddaughter of Nichieiniko Ogasawara, the 12th priest of Murakumo Gosho Zuiryuji-temple, who was the elder sister of Tadamune Ogasawara, the 32nd and former master of the Ogasawara Family. After studying abroad in England and graduating from Sacred Heart Professional Training College, Keishosai became the master of Ogasawararyu-reihou (Ogasawara decorum school) in 1996. She is a visiting professor at Seitoku University and Seitoku University Junior College. She is the author of many books, and does training and gives lectures throughout Japan.

デザイン
文京図案室

イラスト
市村譲

翻訳
板井由紀

翻訳監修
ランディー・チャネル宗榮

Design
Bunkyo-zuan-shitsu

Illustration
Joe Ichimura

Translation
Yuki Itai

Translation supervisor
Randy Channnell Soei

外国人とわかりあうために
英語で伝える日本のマナー

2020年10月14日　初版発行

著者
小笠原敬承斎

発行者
納屋嘉人

発行所
株式会社 淡交社
本社 〒603-8588京都市北区堀川通鞍馬口上ル
　　営業 075-432-5151　編集 075-432-5161
支社 〒162-0061東京都新宿区市谷柳町39-1
　　営業 03-5269-7941　編集 03-5269-1691
　　www.tankosha.co.jp

印刷・製本
中央精版印刷株式会社

Manners and conventions of daily life in Japan
By Keishosai Ogasawara

This book was published in 2020 by Tankosha Publishing Co.,Ltd.